STEP INTO YOUR BEST

LIFE

Visionary Insight
PRESS

Endorsements

What does it take to step into your best life? The willingness to choose to think, feel, and behave differently. The authors in this book will inspire you with stories of how they made those choices, leaving behind lives that were too small. They share their emotional journeys as well as ideas and techniques that will inspire you to make brave choices for the life you were born to live.

Patricia J. Crane, Ph.D.
Heal Your Life® Trainer, Speaker
Author, *Ordering from the Cosmic Kitchen:*
The Essential Guide to Powerful, Nourishing Affirmations
www.drpatriciacrane.com

What an incredible collection of inspiring chapters, each offering different metaphysical concepts. I learned a lot, and this is what I do for a living!

Dick Sutphen
Author, *Soul Agreements*
http://www.richardsutphen.com

As you read the compelling stories of the contributing authors you can't help but feel more hopeful and engaged about your own personal life. There are many tools offered throughout the book to assist you in your journey up the vibrational ladder. I believe Step Into Your Best Life is essential reading for anyone who is seeking out better relationships – not only with others, but also with themselves.

Kenneth L. Peplow, M.S.

This book is a collection of stories expressed from the heart of each writer. Each author shares their personal wisdom of how they overcame adversity by finally discovering their inner power and beauty, which allowed them to make a transformative breakthrough into the life they were born to live! This collection is a guide for everyone who wishes to reclaim their inner power and to experience true freedom and joy! It is about leaving the darkness of self bondage to old belief and fear patterns, and then harnessing courage to step into the Light!

Joy McMahon
Author, *Ageless At 75*
Spiritual Mentor and Numerologist
http://www.joymcmahon.com

All of the stories in this book reflect 'ordinary' people who have identified a pattern, faced the situation and moved on. Their stories can give you the inspiration and tools to deal with the crises currently manifesting in your life.

The authors address the quandaries related to how we think others view us and how we view ourselves. These insightful stories provide the tools and invite you to bring yourself back into clear focus.

Verity Dawson
Licenced Heal Your Life® Teacher, Heal Your Life® News and Inspirations Editor
Reiki, Sekhem and Karuna Master
www.CaribHolisticInsights.com

As published authors, we feel honored to write an endorsement for this compilation book which is a breath of fresh air: Light and airy, yet to the point and consistent with an attitude of helping our fellow man.

We particularly enjoyed the differing views and personal stories from each author, each displaying a thread of commonality. Best of all was the good feeling and glimmer of hope that there are lifelines available for a vast variety of problems and situations occurring in the lives of common ordinary people. The resource list of organizations along with the ways to contact them shows that there are people who care and that they are approachable.

We would urge anyone interested in bettering their lives to not only purchase a copy for themselves, but to purchase several more as gifts to assist those in need. Everyone has in some way been touched by at least one of these things in their own life, and now, there is hope, help, and understanding available.

Skip and Sharon Leingang
Authors, *We Hear and Speak to Dead People*
physicspectrum@msn.com
www.psychicspectrum.com

As humans it is our birthright to thrive and soar, yet we are seldom told that as we make our way in the world. This book will support anyone on their journey to thriving. It is filled with inspiration to keep us putting one foot in front of the other as we claim our best life.

Juliet Vorster
Speaker, Trainer, Broadcaster
www.ThinkANewYou.co.uk

The moment you start to read Step into Your Best Life you will know that this book celebrates life with a sense of gratitude. Each author has their own unique style of sharing their tools that moved them forward to an understanding that life circumstances happen for their personal growth. This inspirational book will help move you too into the direction of self-acceptance and personal responsibility to create your best life!

Robyn Podboy
Personal Growth Facilitator, Heal Your Life® Workshop Facilitator,
Inspirational Speaker
Author, *Beyond Beautiful, Beautiful Seeds of Change* and
Methods of the Masters
http://shineyourlightnow.com

Step Into Your Best Life, what a great challenge full of potential and possibility. The collection of brilliance is a tool box FOR YOU to be exactly that! Created by respected professionals, visionary authors, parents, life coaches and savvy business persons, this book is a delightful cross-section of triumph and resources.

Within these pages, the uplifting personal stories that most persons can relate to because these folks know what it is like to have been down in dark places, including health, home, workplace and personal challenges, share the secret with you of how they turned life around. In today's world, their chapters align perfectly with what necessary actions worked for them in creating and being in their personal best life ever, and I feel and see their guidance and suggestions will work for many who desire to step into the task and step up the Best Life Ever, For YOU!!

RD Riccoboni
Author, *The Big Picture–The Seven Step Guide For Creative Success In Business*
http://rdriccoboni.com
One of America's favorite artists and mentor to many. Visit his gallery and studio, Beacon Artworks in Old San Diego State Historic Park.
http://beaconartworks.com

To
Vicky

STEP INTO YOUR BEST

LIFE

lots of love

Elizabeth
xoxo

STEP INTO YOUR BEST LIFE

Visionary Insight Press, LLC, P.O. Box 30484, Spokane, WA 99223

Visionary Insight Press, the Visionary Insight Press logo and its individual parts are trademarks of Visionary Insight Press, LLC

Compiled by: Lisa Hardwick and Nancy Newman
Cover Design: Kris Voelker
Editorial Director: Nancy Newman
Project Director: Lisa Hardwick
Special Graphics Consultation: Jeanette Combs

A journey of a
thousand miles
begins with just
one step.

~ LAO TZU

Table of Contents

Foreword

by Sunny Dawn Johnston

As an author, speaker and spiritual teacher, I've spoken to many audiences all over the country on the subject of self-love and healing. I've written a best-selling book, *Invoking The Archangels–A Nine-Step Process to Heal Your Body, Mind and Soul,* and founded Sunlight Alliance, a successful healing center in Glendale, Arizona. All of these stepping stones have provided me an opportunity to teach techniques that help others to release pain and "step" into who they really are ... their divine being.

So, when I was asked to write the foreword to this book, the title, *Step Into Your Best Life*, jumped right out at me. I was excited to read over each individual story, and as I worked my way through the book, a familiar feeling came over me. The words and emotions that were expressed on each page mirrored my own journey, and it is no coincidence that I was asked to support this book.

As I read through the chapters, I found myself relating to many authors' experiences. I'd be crying one minute, and joyous the next. I even found myself saying out loud, "Yes ... that's true," "Yup, I did that, too," or "Wow, that was my first step also."

Photo Credit: Lynn Korf

I was elated to read some of my favorite quotes sprinkled throughout the messages of various authors. Each one provided validation for my own feelings, and they reminded me of the little gems I discovered during my own healing process and that you may discover as well.

You will explore such topics as raising your vibration, discovering the stranger in the mirror, trusting your inner guidance system, choosing a conscious life, and looking beyond your limited thinking. I have taught many of these subjects myself, and while the foundation is the same, the perspective and individual experiences are unique. That is why this book will be a great read for you. Each author shares their own individual perspective and experiences and offers steps and anecdotes that can help YOU step into your best life. I wish I had a book like this to read twenty-five years ago. As a teenager, I struggled with my value. I felt as though I had no purpose or reason to be "here." I was unaware of any books like this one that could help me through my doubts and fears, therefore, I was left with only my thoughts. My thoughts were not kind, nor loving to myself or others. I longed for someone, or something to assure me that my life could get better and to show me some steps to get there. I was looking for some hope, some reason to keep moving. Perhaps you can relate?

If so, then the messages in this book will not only give you hope, but will provide guidance in the next step or steps of your healing process. The stories written on these pages are from everyday people who are living their lives and walking their journey just as you and I. They have had their challenges, upsets, pains, and diseases and through it all, continued living life. Life can be something we "get through," survive, barely exist, or it can be something we choose to LIVE, full out!

If you are ready to live, not just exist ...

If you are ready to thrive, not just survive ...

If you are ready and willing to take the next step ... then you see that the journey to your BEST life is in your hands.

In this book, you will receive step-by-step instructions, affirmations and more to being YOUR journey. Are you ready to step into your best life and live the life you are meant to live? You've already taken the first step, the book is in your hands. Now simply turn the page and begin.

Sunny Dawn Johnston
Author of *Invoking the Archangels–*
A Nine-Step Process to Heal Your Body, Mind and Spirit

sunny@sunnydawnjohnston.com
www.sunnydawnjohnston.com
www.invokingthearchangels.com

Introduction

Lisa Hardwick shares valuable insights on how to raise your vibrations to FEEL GOOD when everything else seems out of control.

Nancy Newman reveals how she overcame the disempowerment thinking learned in her youth by reclaiming her power, and how you can, too.

Sandra Filer encourages us to live our life out loud and to allow our own inner light to shine, by showing us how she now lives life as a Sprinkled Doughnut!

Kailah Eglington teaches us how to overcome the dilemma faced by most women over the age of 50 when discovering the stranger in the mirror.

Shellie Couch gives us advice on the proper tools to pack, a road map and a travel guide for a safe and enjoyable journey of our lives!

Nicole Stevenson urges us to trust our inner guidance system and to embark on an expedition of self empowered realizations to discovering our infinite self.

Tracey Willms Deane recognized that her old habits were literally killing her, and decided that was good incentive to choose to change by choosing a conscious life.

Diane S. Christie found her significance by changing her belief to focus on purpose and deal with obstacles, and as a result received a Governor's Award for Leadership in Management.

Merrill Stanton tells about her personal journey from a diagnosis of colon cancer to embracing her health by choosing a different lifestyle and looking beyond her limited thinking.

Deb Wright learned how to create and be in control of her own life free from constraints, judgment and fear which empowered her to not live her life through others.

Elizabeth Candlish shares how a holiday to Vancouver, Canada became a turning point in her life when she moved from England within two years to have the life she dreamed about.

Dena Deluco will inspire you to walk your path with even more poise and elegance by sharing three epiphanies which will support and serve you on your amazing journey.

David Nixon writes about the night when something as simple as the moon changed the course of his life and encourages you to just feel free to be who you are in this moment.

Tammy Gynell Lagoski uses examples from her own life to show us how we create life on a daily basis to prevail upon life's travails.

Lindsley Silagi offers three steps to create the desired changes in our lives to come into the life we were meant to live.

Mavis Hogan explains how the things you do, the people you know and the places you go are all bricks in your wall of who you become.

Lisa Hardwick

LISA HARDWICK is a best-selling Author, Speaker, Workshop Trainer, Publishing Consultant and an advocate for Self Discovery. She is passionate about sharing tools to empower others to live their best lives.

Lisa lives in the same small university town where she was born, Charleston, Illinois, to be near her three adult sons and their families. After years of extensive travel, Lisa has learned that her treasure always resided where her journey began.

lisa@lisahardwick.com
www.lisahardwick.com

 Good Vibrations

" *I AM strong … I AM doing this … I AM worth it …* " I've been repeating these words for an hour and forty minutes. I continue my mantra of affirmations as I raise my head and see my house approximately an eighth of a mile in the distance. In the region of ninety-five degrees, the sun is beating down on me. It is so bright I can barely see. My clothes are stuck to my body, and I am drenched in hot, sticky wetness. I tug at the pedometer on my waistband, and as I look at the device through squinted eyes, beads of sweat drop from my nose on to the display. I wipe them away and read the numbers: 18,207. "You SO ROCK!" I say to myself out loud with a great big smile and continue to put one foot in front of the other. I had just accomplished 18,207 steps at one time! I chug on my second bottle of water and then pour it over my head.

As my driveway presents itself to me, I slow my pace and walk up to the house feeling exhilarated and accomplished. I plop down on my front porch and stretch my legs way out in front of me. I raise my face skyward to allow the sun to kiss my wet cheeks while I take some deep cleansing breaths. The breeze on my wet skin feels amazing.

At this very moment I am simply in a state of deep gratitude for all things.

It wasn't too long ago when setting a goal to walk *one* mile would have seemed unattainable to me. This day, however, I had completed a *seven* mile goal. To me, this was the equivalent of running the Boston Marathon! This was *"my"* Boston Marathon!

Being Selective With Words And Thoughts

Henry Ford was known for the quote *"If you think you can, or you think you can't, you're right!"* Henry's words resonated with me that day and many days thereafter that personal seven- mile marathon when I would set other positive goals for myself. Words are powerful. Words become thoughts, and since thoughts actually create our lives, I have learned to be *very selective* with the words I say and the thoughts I think.

I wasn't always like this. In fact, I was what many would call a polar opposite of this new way of choosing to live my life. Previously, I was morbidly obese, suffered from severe clinical depression, anxiety attacks and post traumatic stress disorder in addition to being on multiple prescriptions. My words and thoughts were *always* negative. Needless to say, I was not a happy person. Today, my life is obviously quite different.

What Makes A Person Happy?

Allow me to ask a question: How do you think most would answer if you were to ask, "What would make you most happy?" Do you agree that most would say to be wealthy, slim, attractive and successful? I'm certain there would be many who would also say they would be most happy if they were to find the love of their life, to have good things for their family, live in their dream home, take amazing vacations, to have perfect health, etc. But think about this for a moment – Isn't what we all *really* want is to simply "feel good"?

If *you* were to think that to be most happy you would choose for your-self to be thin, rich and with the love of your life, then what you are *actually* saying is it would "feel good" to be thin, rich and in love. Right? So the goal then – is really to "feel good" not necessarily to obtain what we *believe* would make us happy. When I learned this, I realized I had been on the wrong path for far too many years.

When I further obtained the knowledge that our bodies have over seventy-five trillion cells that simultaneously vibrate, and that the higher frequency of vibration we have, the healthier cells we have and the results are that we feel better. So it is apparent that when we feel poorly, our cells are infected by such maladies in our lives like disease, being overweight, depression, anger, etc. In other words, all things we associate with being *negative*. And when we have negativity in our lives, and our cells are vibrating at a low frequency, we then feel depleted and exhausted and the result is we feel bad.

When our lives are filled with love, joy, peace and gratitude, and our mind, body and spirit are in an optimal balance, we are vibrating at a high frequency and we feel good.

Imagine for a moment a time in your life when you felt less than stellar. Now try to recall what thoughts were going through your mind at that time. What were the circumstances? Did you happen to manifest more of the same type of events or people due to the fact you attract what you are? Remember, when you feel bad, you are vibrating at a low level. When you are vibrating at a high level, well, you feel good! So really, the ultimate goal is to learn the tools to vibrate at a higher frequency – not necessarily to win the lottery.

Brilliant And Highly Intelligent Teachers

This information isn't anything new. We have many brilliant and highly intelligent ancestors who have been teaching us for years about the power of thoughts, affirmations and how to live a life vibrating at a higher frequency. For instance, Claude M. Bristol, Napoleon Hill,

Albert Einstein, Dr. David Schwartz, Dean Francis and numerous others, too many to list. These pioneers inspired the teachers we have available to us today such as Louise Hay, Tony Robbins, Sunny Dawn Johnston, Andy Dooley, Michael Tamura and Dr. Wayne Dyer just to name a few. There are an abundance of others, again, too numerous to list, who have made it their life's work to share the teachings with us on how to live our best lives, which in essence, is how to feel good.

The question you may have now is: "How, then, do I raise my frequency to vibrate at a higher level so I feel good?" Ahhh ... and that is the million dollar question, and I'm so glad you asked! If you are wondering how to do just this, then you understand the concept and before long you will be taking the steps to live your best life! Isn't that exciting?! What is even more delightful is there are *many* ways to raise your vibrating frequency!

Move Toward What Feels Good – Move Away From What Does Not

Seems simple, doesn't it? Well actually, it is! The first and most important task we all must do is simply be *aware* of how we are feeling. Many people simply dredge through life not even realizing how they feel. They may have the attitude of: "Well, this is it. This is life. This is all there is." In actuality what they are saying is: "I don't feel good." Because when you "feel good," you say things like: "Life is so good! My life is really great! I'm doing great! I love life! I love people!"

When you become aware of how you feel, simply CHOOSE to move towards thoughts, people and objects that feel good! See, I told you it was simple! Let's say for example you walk past a mirror and glance at yourself. You immediately think: "I look terrible." When your mind chatters with such thoughts, make a conscious choice to conduct a *re-do*! Sure, it's allowed! Why not!? If golf has a mulligan, life can have a re-do! Back up and walk past the mirror again and change your thoughts. "Look at you, girl! You are so fit!" or perhaps "Your hair sure looks beautiful today!"

Another example might be something like when you hear your phone ring and you notice it's from your friend, "Debbie Downer." (Thank goodness for Caller ID!) You have a CHOICE to not answer. You additionally have the option to pick up the phone and dial "Fantastic Faye" instead! Be aware of your vibrations! Be responsible for raising them! As you continue to practice moving toward what feels good and moving away from what does not, you will notice you are starting to feel good all the time without even having to think about it! Soon it will be automatic.

> ❧ It's the repetition of affirmations that leads to belief. And once that belief becomes a deep conviction, things begin to happen.
>
> ~ CLAUDE M. BRISTOL

Releasing What We No Longer Need

One of my most favorite affirmations I use consistently is: *"I release what I no longer need."* It is invaluable in many areas of my life, including my thoughts, things, people and my body. When I am at a place where I don't "feel good," then this is a sign to me that I need to release something. When I become aware of what that something is, I make a conscious choice to use this affirmation over and over until whatever needs to be released is gone. When I am at an event and I feel the energy vibration around me isn't what makes me feel my best, I say to myself: *"I release this energy and find a higher vibration now."* Or if I am feeling sluggish due to not eating the foods that are most nutritious for me and/or not being as active as when I feel my best, I use the affirmation: *"I release what my body no longer needs."*

Yet there's more … with each affirmation I then trust and move toward the path my inner self guides me to take to release what is needed to discharge. And once I let go, I immediately feel my vibrations rise to a higher level.

 Any idea, plan, or purpose may be placed in the mind through repetition of thought.

~ NAPOLEON HILL

It's Only Contrast

I recall a time when I was working in a profession that seemed to suffocate any chance of living with a high frequency vibration. Every single morning when I would drive into the parking lot, I felt like I could barely breathe. During this time I was in the process of learning about high and low vibrations, and I would feel defeated in my vision to "feel good" every time I walked through my office door. Upon speaking to a mentor about this situation, she gently gifted me with, *"Lisa, it's only contrast. Contrast is simply a situation that assists with reminding you of what you don't want. It is a gift! So as you move toward your vision of living your best life, embrace this 'contrast' now and thank it for showing you what you don't want – so you don't forget! Also, contrast further helps by giving you a clear vision of what you DO want so you can continue to move toward that goal."*

So today, when I find myself in a situation that is obviously at a low frequency vibration, I realize it is simply contrast. I acknowledge it, thank it for the reminder of what I don't desire, and then I search my inner guidance for a better choice, a better vision, and take steps to move toward that better choice for me and a higher level of vibrations.

 The ancestor of every action is a thought.

~ RALPH WALDO EMERSON

Visualize To Materialize

I teach and practice guided visualization meditation. However, you don't necessarily need to jump on a plane, fly to my location and set aside an entire hour to reap the benefits of raising your vibrations through a formal presentation exercise. In fact, you can raise your vibration level in as little as seventeen minutes simply by focusing on a thought that brings you joy! Remember the last time you genuinely enjoyed yourself? Perhaps you were at an event with your best friends having dinner, drinking wine and laughing. Maybe it was on a beach with your partner, and you were soaking up the sun while feeling the breeze dance over your body. Or perhaps it was when you accomplished something special. Whatever it was, you can choose to relax your body and your mind and go to that place in your thoughts whenever you decide and relive those moments. When you choose to guide your thoughts toward this vision, your vibrating frequency will automatically increase!

Throughout my week I am always off to some other place or experience. I travel all over the world to places like Jamaica, St. Thomas and the Bahamas. Other times I am reliving a special event. Why not? Why not take the time to deeply focus if you know it's going to make you "feel good"? It will not cost you a cent and the rewards are tantamount to hitting the lottery!

Another visualization tool I use quite often is goal setting. I will focus on the goal and then I will focus on where I am currently and see myself taking each step toward my intention until I reach it. I picture what I am wearing, who I will be meeting along the way, where I will be going, conversations I will be having, anything related to my vision. I picture it in my mind and experience it as if it was actually happening right at that moment! Then (and this is the best part), I visualize reaching that goal and experience every sensation imaginable as if I had already obtained it. I "feel" it! I "live" it! It becomes part of me.

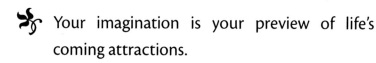 Your imagination is your preview of life's coming attractions.

~ ALBERT EINSTEIN

Shake Your Groove Thing

I really love to dance. In my mind, I dance like those cool, young, hip-hop dancers you see surrounding Usher in his music videos. But the truth is, I have very little rhythm or trendy moves. However, truth be told, I don't care. I put on the latest hits and get up and do my thing. Music and dancing are *extremely* powerful in raising your vibrations! And if I have an audience watching me while I am showing them my latest moves, we can always count on bringing laughter into the mix.

Keep in mind, laughter is one of *the* most powerful tools for raising vibrations. Have you ever been in a group of people where one person tells a joke and everyone laughs, but then someone's laugh is even *funnier* than the joke? Now *that* is funny! I've never walked out of a comedy club in a bad mood. Have you?

At the height of laughter, the universe is flung into a kaleidoscope of new possibilities.

~ JEAN HOUSTON

Best And Highest Good

Take a moment and put down this book. Next, spread out your arms as wide as you can at your sides. Make a big "T" with your body. Raise your face to the sky, smile and repeat: "All for my best and highest good." Visualize glittery, sparkling gold light entering your body through your heart and filling your entire being with Universal loving energy. Visualize your vibration level rising and trust that all from this moment on will be ALL for your BEST and HIGHEST GOOD.

When we practice affirmative meditation tools such as this, we are energized, and it becomes easier to take the steps toward what is ideal for living our best life. We are able to trust and know that all of the decisions we will be making on that given day will be divinely guided.

I begin each day by speaking these words. There are times within my day when I am working with a team on a common vision that I choose to take a moment, open my arms and say, "This vision or something *even* better for my highest good and the good of all involved." I love to send these messages out into the Universe, and I equally love to assist with raising the vibrations of the team members I am associated with!

Can you imagine doing this in your place of employment? You wouldn't have to do it front of your co-workers – you could simply take a break and do it where no one was watching. This works especially well if someone is irritating you and your co-workers. Simply send some loving energy and do your part to raise the vibration frequency of the offending party. Perhaps if s/he felt better, then maybe *the team* would feel better.

I will tell you though, no matter if they change their irritating behavior or not, you now know that if they are vibrating at a lower frequency, they are in obvious pain from some type of affliction from negativity in their cells that is affecting their quality of life. Be patient with them. Most people who are at a low level frequency just need a little more patience, love and hope. Perhaps some day when the time is right, you might share with them some of the tools you have learned to raise your own vibrations! Then, everyone wins!

At this moment, I set an intention that you and I practice being truly aware of how we *feel*. Further, I affirm that you and I make it a mandatory responsibility on a daily basis to utilize the tools we know for raising our own vibration frequency level, and when the time is right, perhaps share these tools with others so they, too, can "feel good."

You might even choose to do what I am going to go do right now. I am going to turn up some awesome tunes that have a really funky beat and practice some new cool dance moves! Join me?

Dedicated to the amazing students, mentors and teachers I have been fortunate enough to have been connected to on this incredible life journey and to the many more I have yet to meet.

Many thanks for the support of friends, family and colleagues with special mention of my parents, Monte and Linda Nugent, and my sons, Christopher Miller, Aaron Miller and Austin Miller. My heart is overflowing with gratitude for each and every one of you.

~ Lisa Hardwick

Nancy Newman

NANCY NEWMAN is a licensed Heal Your Life® Coach, Workshop Facilitator and Teacher with a private practice, Mindful Wellness, in Spokane, Washington. She is also an author and speaker empowering people throughout the world to live their authentic lives by sharing her personal stories, facilitating workshops, and teaching the tools for healing, loving yourself and discovering the peace within.

Nancy is also a certified Reiki Master, Reflexologist, and registered Master Toe Reader. She enjoys traveling to Portland, Oregon to spend time with her son, daughter-in-law and grandbaby, London Ava.

nancy@yourmindfulwellness.com
www.yourmindfulwellness.com

Your Power Is In Choice

 Any change, any loss, does not make us victims. Others can shake you, surprise you, or disappoint you, but they can't prevent you from moving on. No matter where you are in life, no matter what your situation, you can always do something. On every turn of life, you will always have a choice. And that choice can be your power.

~ BLAINE LEE

My Moment Of Choice

The insulting and hostile words were being hurled at me like stones from a catapult while I futilely tried to dodge the painful blows. Each attempted explanation of my actions or the thinking behind the action, was rejected and rebuffed with: "That's not true!" Or, "I don't want to hear that." I could feel the adrenaline surging, causing my whole body to shake. I had to put down the keys I was holding because they were clattering in my hands. But I was reacting as I had been taught and was being a "good girl" by not saying anything back ... that is, until he took two steps toward me. That was my moment of choice.

A Good Girl

My whole life has revolved around being a "good girl." I was raised in the South where authority figures have the final say. One of the things I was taught was that no matter what was said or done to you, you didn't talk back – not to parents, teachers, doctors, policemen, bosses, husbands, older family members, etc. These people were accorded respect whether they had earned it or not.

And, if you were a woman, there was also the rule that you did not talk back to men. *Ever.* Back in the 1950's, in the South particularly, men were also considered authority figures. Men were able to do what they wanted and say what they wanted, with no repercussions, simply because they were men.

I took this rule and all the rest of my training to heart, and I was a *REALLY* good girl! But, oh my – these teachings which were instilled in me as a young girl would deliver some "interesting" situations to me the rest of my life. Even in my 60's, I was still being a good girl.

Belief In Un-Deservedness

When I was a child, there were men in my life who molested and sexually abused me. As I became a teenager, there were incidents of date rape. In my late teens, I married a verbally abusive and physically intimidating man. As an adult, I seemed to "attract" male bosses who continued the verbal abuse and intimidation. Clearly there was a pattern here, and I would wonder to myself why I "always" seemed to attract these types of men. I thought I just had bad luck.

Little did I realize that all those years I was making a CHOICE about how I lived my life, a choice about the things that happened in my life, and a choice as to the people who populated my life. Yes, a CHOICE! Even a subconscious choice is still a choice!

Why would anyone CHOOSE, whether consciously or subconsciously, to surround themselves with people who mistreat them, and with experiences that are not joy-affirming or life-affirming?

It wasn't until I was in my 40's that I learned part of the answer! But it wouldn't be until my 60's that I really began to put that learning to work. I learned that other people in our lives are a reflection of how we feel about ourselves. By subconsciously (or consciously) believing we deserve this type of treatment, we attract people and experiences into our lives which validate our own beliefs about ourselves!

This belief of un-deservedness begins when we accept the statements and actions of others as our own truth! Have you ever seen a small baby who didn't believe they deserved EVERYTHING? It's true – what baby or toddler doesn't let you know, in no uncertain terms, when they wholeheartedly BELIEVE they deserve the toy, or their favorite treat, or to stay up later? They have not yet accepted someone else's truth about their deservability.

Then, at some point, someone in our life told us that we weren't good enough. Maybe it was a teacher in school. Maybe it was a parent. Maybe it was another child. Maybe it was several different people. But at some time at least one person told us that we weren't good enough, and we accepted their truth as our own! We made a *CHOICE* to accept their truth about us as our own truth. And once that belief takes hold, it spreads to all areas of our lives.

Disempowerment Thinking

The thought that we "aren't good enough" is so ingrained in our sub-conscious, that our conscious mind skips over that as we think to our-selves, "This house deal is too good to be true, it will never happen." Or, "I'll never be able to get a job." Or, "I'll never get a raise." Or, "I'll probably fail this test." Or, "I'll never get well." Or, "I'll never find the love of my life." Implied in all those statements is the continuing sub-conscious thought: " … because I'm not good enough."

This feeling of not being good enough is so pervasive that Louise Hay, one of the early pioneers in the mind-body-spirit connection, has said that every person she has worked with had this belief. In my work-shops and with my clients, I have worked with people from around the world, and have come to believe that the feeling of "not being good enough," is a UNIVERSAL feeling that crosses all countries and all cultures.

I believe in the Law of Attraction. In other words, "thought becomes form," or "life follows thought." By believing the false truth: "I'm not good enough," you are creating a negative outcome as a result of your fears and past conditioning by accepting the false truth of others as your own truth. This is also known as "Disempowerment Thinking." And when you have accepted this false truth as your own truth, you attract to you people and events that will validate and perpetuate your belief.

Rather than staying stuck in disempowerment thinking, you can CHOOSE to think empowering thoughts which can turn your neg-ative outcomes into positive outcomes. No longer do you need to be a victim of your "stinkin' thinking" and attract negative life experi-ences and unwanted physical symptoms which simply reinforce your belief in not being good enough.

Empowerment Thinking

So, how do you turn things around? Can it really be as easy as just changing your thoughts? Yes, it can. It is an easy answer, but sometimes not so easy to actually put into action. One reason is because your subconscious beliefs will continue to try to sabotage you: "This will never work; it's too easy! If it were that easy, why isn't everyone doing it?"

Knowing that you can create the life of your dreams and the physical experience you desire is the easy part. *Working* to do it is quite another. In order for the belief of deservedness to be able to replace the feeling of un-deservedness, it is necessary to do a lot of work on learning to love yourself. As I said, although I learned that I could create my own life in my 40's, I wasn't able to actually put that into action until my 60's!

One of the ways to begin empowerment thinking is by changing your self-talk. I've heard it said that the average human has 80,000 thoughts per day, and 98% of these are negative! How can you ever feel that you are good enough, when you are thinking 78,400 negative thoughts a day by constantly telling yourself things such as, "I'm too fat." Or, "I'm too old." Or, "Geez, that was really stupid." Or, "I always screw things up." Or, "I'll never get ahead." Or, [fill in the blank with your most common negative statement to yourself]. Self-criticism will lock us into the very patterns we are trying to change.

> ❧ Every time you are tempted to react in the same old way, ask if you want to be a prisoner of the past or a pioneer of the future.
>
> ~ DEEPAK CHOPRA

How much better would you feel by telling yourself, "I am always doing the best I can." Or, "My income is constantly increasing." Or, "You are really smart at these things." Or, "I love how you get things right." Do you ever compliment yourself? If you've been criticizing yourself for years, as Dr. Phil says: "How's that been working for ya?" Try complimenting yourself instead, nurturing yourself – LOVING yourself, exactly the way you are right now. To love yourself means never, ever criticizing yourself again. Starting right now!

 I'm encouraging you to initiate a habit of choosing thoughts and ideas that support feeling good and powerful, that elevate you to a higher level of consciousness.

~ DR. WAYNE DYER

Loving yourself also means accepting yourself EXACTLY as you are right now. This very minute. Loving yourself at your current weight, your current income level, whether you've achieved your dreams or not. Love yourself right now. You can begin by saying to yourself: "I love you exactly the way you are!" This statement is even more powerful when you say it to yourself while gazing into your own eyes in a mirror.

Release The Past

In addition to loving ourselves unconditionally, it is important to release the past. We cannot change the past, we can only create our present and our future. If our thoughts and beliefs create the way we experience our lives and our physical bodily expression of life, then your current experience is the result of the thoughts and beliefs from the last minute, the last hour, the last day, the last week, the last year.

Even though we can't change our past, we can change our *thoughts* about the past thereby creating a different future! We can re-write our story.

✼ Refuse to allow any thoughts based on your past to define you.

~ DR. WAYNE DYER

By persisting to think about past hurts and perceived wrongs either consciously or subconsciously, we are now continuing to inflict the hurt on ourselves and accepting the opinions and actions of others as our truth. We repeat the story over and over and over so often, we accept it as our belief, and we live our lives as if it were true. That is when it becomes our false truth and our reality.

By continuing to let others occupy space in our heads, we allow them to determine our thoughts and our truths! They are continuing to hurt us even when the criticism, judgment or abuse has ended. They may even be dead, but we hear *their* truths coming out of our mouths or in our heads as our thoughts.

By rewriting the story, I'm not suggesting that we pretend things didn't happen, or that we change history. But what if we could change the RESULT of that history? What if we could change our thoughts about this false truth of ourselves that we've accepted as true based on the actions or beliefs of others?

✼ A belief is only a thought, and thoughts can be changed!

~ LOUISE HAY

The point of power is right now, this very minute! By changing your thoughts, changing your self-talk and accepting yourself exactly the way you are, you can begin the process of creating your next minute, your next hour, your next week, your next month, your next year!

A part of the training to become certified to teach the Louise Hay philosophy was writing down some of our thoughts and beliefs from the past. One of the things I wrote was: "No one wants to hear what I have to say." I thought I truly believed that. But it was not MY belief. It was a false truth of others that I had accepted as my own. In my own childhood, I was constantly told, "Nancy, be quiet." "Nancy, don't ask so many questions." "Nancy, no one wants to hear what you have to say."

When we were encouraged at the training to rewrite our story and turn that belief around, I wrote: "I am a writer, teacher and healer who creates and shares programs all over the world that bring joy, healing and peace to others."

I embraced this new truth. I felt so good when I affirmed this new statement every day as I continued to work on changing my thoughts and beliefs surrounding my deservedness and on loving myself. Within six months, I was writing a chapter for a collaborative book; within a year, I was an editor for a publishing company and an anchor writer for an on-line women's magazine; and within two years, I was a co-owner of a publishing company helping others to bring their words of healing to people all around the planet. Changing my belief and embracing my new truth certainly changed what I attracted into my life, and it can work for you, too.

To assist in this process, I highly recommend the books: *You Can Heal Your Life* by Louise Hay, and *Ordering From the Cosmic Kitchen* by Dr. Patricia Crane, as positive steps to change your thoughts and to learn how to create positive, nurturing affirmations.

Standing In Your Power

Returning to my moment of choice, as I stood there listening to the verbal tirade accompanied by threatening physical gestures, I simultaneously heard my mother's voice in my head: "Nancy, don't you dare talk back! He's a man, *AND* he's your boss. You are lucky to even have a job in this economy, much less one that pays so well. Don't you dare jeopardize that!" I felt powerless and helpless – not only was I dealing with someone standing in front of me intimidating and abusing me, I was dealing with the ingrained messages from my dead mother that I had accepted as my truth! What a dilemma: I couldn't continue to be a "good girl" if I defied my mother and my false beliefs.

At one point, I actually said to the man in front of me: "Please stop yelling at me. This isn't fair, you have all the power." And at that time, I thought he had the power simply because he was an authority figure and a man. But as he advanced those two steps toward me, I recognized that his only power was the power I had given away based on my past teachings and beliefs.

> ❧ The most common way people give up their power is thinking they don't have any.
>
> ~ ALICE WALKER

In that moment I realized I had two options: I could continue to give him my power by remaining silent and being a good girl as I had done with all the other abusive men in my life, or I could make the choice to take my own power back and no longer allow myself to be a victim. I could believe that I *DESERVED* to be treated with dignity and respect. That moment was a point of power: I could choose to remain silent and continue the false belief system, or I could risk choosing a new thought and belief and change my future. The choice was hinged in the point of power in that moment.

And the day came when the risk to remain tight in a bud was more painful than the risk it took to blossom.

~ ANAIS NIN

As I embraced the point of power in that moment, I made the *CHOICE* to stand up for myself and not be a victim. In that moment, I changed my past thoughts and beliefs that a woman could never talk back to a man, that an authority figure was always right and you had to do what they said, to the thought and belief that I deserved to be treated with dignity and respect, and I did not have to remain silent! I was not willing to endure and accept that abusive treatment any longer from anyone, no matter the cost. As I began to defend myself, raising my voice louder and louder, I began to feel more and more empowered.

Was I afraid? You bet! But the fear wasn't of HIM, the fear was the unknown – what would happen if I changed the beliefs and teachings of 63 years? Would the earth open up and swallow me? Believe me, the exaggerated thoughts of calamitous results were what had previously prevented me from changing the actions and beliefs of a lifetime. It would take an enormous leap of faith to find the courage to risk choosing a different path.

Courage to overcome fear can be deceiving. The key is realizing that courage isn't as much about overcoming fear as it is about not settling for less than you deserve. Overcoming fear to find your courage is like Dorothy in the Wizard of Oz with her ruby slippers, I had the courage and the power all along, I just didn't realize it. Dorothy just needed to click her heels; I just needed to decide that I DESERVED to be treated with dignity and respect by everyone, including myself! I had to love myself more than my false beliefs.

Look for the gifts in everything, especially when you are facing what appears to be a negative situation. Everything that we attract causes us to grow, which means that ultimately everything is for our own good. Adjusting to a new path and a new direction will require new qualities and strengths, and these qualities are always exactly what we need to acquire in order to accomplish the great things ahead in our life.

~ DINA KHALIL

My choice to stand up for myself was a risk in more ways than one, and came at the cost of my job. But my choice in that moment gave me the power of knowing that I could defend myself and stand up to an angry, intimidating male presence, which reclaimed the power that I had been giving away for most of my life. I absolutely realized in that moment of choice that I was putting my job in jeopardy. After all, he was one of my bosses, but that did not give him the right to treat me in an abusive manner. Any concern over risking my job paled in comparison to allowing myself to be treated in such an unacceptable, disrespectful manner. And with that choice in that moment, I also gave myself the gift of freedom.

 She went out on a limb, had it break off behind her, and realized she could fly.

~ KOFI YAMADA

I am now free to step forward into my best life! I am creating the life I have dreamed about for several years, and I'm now living my passion. Every day I get to do what "lights my fire." I experience joy every single day. No, getting to this point didn't happen overnight, and no, it wasn't easy. It was a process that began years ago when I knew I was here to be of service to the planet and knew that to do so effectively, I had to begin clearing away a lot of old stuff. Since then, I've done a lot of healing work, which has been painful at times and other times exhilarating. But it was always with the knowledge that I was creating my dream life – that I was putting in the building blocks to be the person I wanted to be – the one I believed I had been BORN to be!

In order to make the choice I did, I needed to have done the healing work in order to be able to believe I did not have to "settle" for disrespectful and abusive treatment. I needed to be able to embrace the belief that I was worthy. I needed to be willing to love myself. This enabled me to find the courage to proclaim to the world and myself that I deserved to be treated with dignity and respect.

What are your thoughts right now? Is this a thought you want creating your future? Are you creating a future resulting from thoughts of love, peace, joy and self-approval, or a future resulting from thoughts of criticism, anger, resentment and guilt? The best gift you will ever give yourself is the gift of healing, loving yourself and discovering the peace within.

Your power to create your life is in your choices right now. Make the choice to change your thoughts and beliefs, and change your life for the better! Remember, the Point of Power is right now, this very second! What are you waiting for? Why wait another minute? Step into your best life now.

Dedicated to Dan, Jenni & London. I love all of you more than life itself. And to my "twin," you know who you are, I am so grateful that we literally ran into one another on that street corner, turned and together walked into the rest of our life adventures!

Thanks to my many teachers and mentors for helping me on this amazing path. I have been fortunate to meet many others who knowingly and unknowingly helped guide me to my path. A special thanks to the law firm partner who unwittingly convinced me that my power had always been mine, I had just been giving it away. Thanks to him, I am now living the life of my dreams!

~ Nancy Newman

Sandra Filer

SANDRA J. FILER, MBA, is a gifted artist, speaker, author, beauty consultant, and licensed Heal Your Life® Coach & Workshop Leader. Sandra is also actively involved with the Woman Within Organization and the Empowered Girls Alliance. She is passionate about empowering people to live happy, healthy, and love-filled lives through coaching and workshops.

Sandra lives on a quiet lantern lit street with her love, Mr. Kim Coffman, and six fabulous felines. She enjoys her family, friends, having fun, creating art, being in nature, and escaping to her favorite island in Florida.

diosafeliz@hotmail.com
www.thehappygoddess.com

❧ Living Out Loud:
The Story Of The Sprinkled Donut

"Sing Sandi! Sing for your grandma!" This is the joyful encouragement I received as a wee three-year-old, from my grandma, Sophia. My grandma would invite me to climb up on the dining room table to sing for her, my aunt, and my uncles. Gleefully, wee little Sandi would sing. The song of choice was *The Yellow Rose of Texas*.

On top of that table, I was a twinkling star. I was a delight to my family. I was a brightly shining beam of light. As I would share my song, with great enthusiasm, my grandma and the other family members would clap, smile, giggle, and acknowledge my talent. It felt invigorating. I was living out loud.

I can recall many stories of myself as a small child. Before I share these stories, I will preface it all with the fact that I was born to two parents who love me dearly. Over the course of this story, I will share some things that *may* seem unloving. However, I now know that nothing was ever done intentionally, and that my mother and father were always doing the best they could do with their respective skill sets. After all, children do not come with an operating manual.

We lived in Flint, Michigan. My father worked on the line at General Motors. He "worked very hard to put food on our table." My mother worked as a secretary at a bank for several years after I was born.

Interestingly, it would turn out to be the same bank at which I would unknowingly begin my own banking career.

My mother worked until the day she arrived at my grandma's house to pick me up, only to find me crying that I did not want to leave. Grandma's house was a whole lot of fun. I was a twinkling little star there.

Grandma Sophia taught wee little Sandi how to plant a rooted snip of the plant. After the instructions were given, being the diligent little student that she was, Sandi made a go of it. Then, she proudly displayed her result. I can still remember the laughter. Rather than plant the roots in the dirt, in my youthful innocence, I planted the little rooted cutting upside down. Later my grandma would tell that story amidst laughter and with her eyes sparkling.

My mother shared that there was a time when I entered the kitchen and proclaimed my desire to catch a bird. Evidently, my mother was very busy but I continually inquired about catching a bird. In her exasperation, she finally said, "If you take a salt shaker outside with you, and you sprinkle the tail of a bird, you will catch one." Well, guess what? Smart little Sandi caught one.

I was a creative child. This quality would prove to be quite beneficial, especially since I was raised in a household where money was tight. Using my creativity, the dolls would be clothed in doilies and wash towels. Yarn would be a fancy accessory. Dollhouses would be crafted from boxes. Yes, I lived in an imaginary world where common things would transform themselves into purposeful creations.

One day, I can remember "dressing up." I found a pair of socks and a few square building blocks. Carefully, the building blocks were inserted into my socks to create "high heels." Next, I added a parasol (every day ordinary umbrella) to the ensemble and took my little self out the front door to the sidewalk. On that sidewalk, on a beautifully sunny day, I twirled around singing and playing ... right in front of "the neighbors." Gasp!

Very quickly, I was informed that it was time to come into the house. I was told that my father was upset. He was concerned about "what the neighbors would think." This would be one of my very first memories of my inner light being dimmed.

Meanwhile, over at my other grandma's house, I was appearing in my own show. My Grandma Lois loved having a granddaughter. Like Sophia, she would encourage me to be me. At Grandma Lois' house, I would escape into a fantasy world of dressing up like a diva. My grandma had dresser drawers filled with jewelry. She had closets full of shoes – of every color imaginable. Additionally, she had mink coats that she was willing to let me wear. It was a place of little girl bliss. Hours were spent there in the imaginary and magical "dress-up" world. Now, this would all happen until my grandpa would come home. Grandpa didn't allow me to play with the "good things."

Still, when I was at my Grandma Lois' house, I could get whatever I wanted. Or so my mother said. As the years would continue, this became a problem for my mother. Suddenly, I had a new nickname: Queenie. My mother would continuously state (in a sarcastic manner), "Whatever Queenie wants, Queenie gets."

Suddenly, I – the apple of my grandmothers' collective eyes – had a label. You see, my mother and my father were not very happy. They had married very young because of a pregnancy. That pregnancy terminated. Yet, very soon thereafter, they were pregnant again with me. Being the first born of three, I got a lot of attention. My father took me almost everywhere that he went. With the ever-increasing stress of a not-so-happy marriage and so much attention on little Sandi, (instead of my mother), it is my assessment that my mother grew somewhat resentful of me. In her frustration, she would "let me know" just how spoiled I had become. In that "letting me know," my inner light was being dimmed.

During my early elementary school days, I befriended children who were being teased by others. I often trusted the bully and got myself into trouble. I was once coaxed to climb down into a muddy hole by a bunch of bullies. They promised to help me up. It was a dare! I did as they requested, only to be left in the hole to climb my way out. The hole was deep as it was for the foundation of a new home being constructed. I was wearing my brand new Easter shoes and coat, as I dug my way to the surface. It was a very scary experience. I was betrayed by the bullies and landed myself in big trouble with my mother. I was late, and I had ruined my new Easter shoes and coat. This memory has been preserved by a Polaroid photo taken of "bad little Sandi."

I realize now that I made many choices because of my underlying desire to be liked. At an early age, I began practicing the fine art of pleasing to gain the acceptance of others.

Despite any limitations placed on me, I had moments when I would make the valiant effort to add the sparkle.

Once when I was in the 3rd grade, I remember sneaking pantyhose and wearing them to class only to have a boy tease me and say, "Who do you think you are, Mrs. Nixon?" Another time, I snuck a multi-strand of crystals to school to wear in my class photo. My mother was not happy because I ventured away from what I was "supposed" to wear in the photograph. Yet another time, I tucked a multi-colored scarf in my pocket, to once again bedazzle my outfit for the school photos. That did not go over well either.

In high school, I really strived to do anything and everything that I could to please everyone. I was a Girl Scout, sang in choir, performed on the Pom Pom squad and, of course, had to be the Captain. As if that wasn't enough, I also bowled on the bowling team. This is something that I did because my father was (and still is) a really good bowler, and I wanted him to be proud of me. I took it one step farther at the ripe old age of 14 and decided to become the "girlfriend" of the boy whose parents owned the bowling alley. My dad was happy because he got to bowl for free.

My pleasing behavior went far beyond the need to please my parents. I now wanted acceptance from the boys at school. I recall one day at school vividly well. One of the boys was wearing a flannel, button-down shirt. He was pulling it down on the bottom so that it was taut across his chest. He announced to the entire class, "Look at me, my chest looks like Sandi's." Ouch! That really hurt. After that incident, there was a new focus on my boobs. Of course, they were never big enough or good enough. However, they could be used as a tool in the effort to be liked.

It is amazing when I think about how I compromised myself to gain the attention of a boy. I believe this is why I am so passionate now about instilling in young girls how "perfect" they are, exactly as they are. How did I compromise myself? Let me share one example.

There was a boy on the high school football and basketball teams. I thought he was really cute, and I wanted him to like me. As fate would have it, we were seated next to each other in accounting class. It just so happened that I was very good at accounting, and he was not. I decided that the way to his heart was to allow him to cheat off of my paper. And, if that wasn't enough, not only did I allow him to cheat off my paper, but I also unbuttoned my blouse so he could see my breast.

It amazes me to think that I stooped so low to be liked. However, low self-esteem can create behaviors that we later regret ... or, at least, have to live with. Clearly, my self-esteem was low because none of my achievements were ever enough.

I can remember being invited to Honor's night before my high school graduation. Upon receiving the invitation, I said to my parents that it must be a mistake. I was terrified that I would get to the awards ceremony only to be left without anything. My mother called the school and confirmed that I had indeed, won an award. It was an artist's award.

During these years, there was bickering in our home. My mother and father grew farther and farther apart. There was a lot of anger. There were a lot of names being called. It was a stressful place where no one was pleasing anyone. All I wanted was to run away and find a happy home.

I landed my first job in the banking industry at the age of 17. I was still in high school, and my friend and I did it as a co-op job. It provided so much freedom for me. I felt a sense of belonging. It was also really cool because my friend drove a Camaro. We would ride with our windows open and the music playing loudly.

This job would be followed up with another job at a different bank. A whole new world began to open up for me. I was again a star in my own show. My boss was a fantastic mentor. She would push me and teach me and also correct inappropriate behavior. Through her guidance, I dumped my high school boyfriend. Finally! It was hard to let go of the "bowler" because it made my father so happy.

I loved working at the bank. Every day, I would dress up in totally coordinated outfits. On Fridays, I dressed up especially pretty because it was the day that the factories would let out, and all the men would come in to cash their paychecks.

Around this same period, my parents' marriage finally ended. My mother was in college studying to be a nurse. One day at the bank, one of her professors visited my teller window. After she looked at my name, she asked, "Oh, are you Dolores' daughter?" The answer to that question was yes.

Later I learned that the professor saw my mother on the following day and said, "Wow, I met your daughter at the bank. She is so pretty and dresses up so colorfully." To which my mother said, "Oh, yes, that is my Sandi. She is the sprinkled donut, and I am just the plain one."

As you can well imagine by now, it didn't always feel so good to be the sprinkled donut. After all, all I really ever wanted was to be liked. So, as time went on, I continued to dim my light. Those sprinkles seemed to get in the way!

While gainfully employed, I decided to save money to rent an apartment and purchase a new car. I was on track to live that happy life that I left home to live. This dream included the fairy tale of being whisked away by a knight in shining armor.

Well, he whisked me away all right ... however, his horse was a skateboard. My "knight" was a bank customer. He showed interest in me by smiling through the vestibule window when he would get cash from the ATM. When I worked outside in the drive-through building, he would skateboard by (with his dog). I was intrigued. One day he called. Nine months later, we were married.

During our six years together, I was never "enough." I can remember once early on, he took me out to play Frisbee. He would launch the disc far away from me so that I had to run. In answer to the question of why he did that, he said, "To whittle you down." When we divorced, he actually told me that I was like a diamond in the rough before I met him. Obviously, I attracted this man into my life because my self-esteem was so low.

Not to be thwarted, I met yet another man that showed interest. Once again, the meeting place was at the bank. Needy for love, I immediately fell for him. After a short courtship, he moved in with me. This relationship would prove to be a competition for who could get the highest level of degree and move up the corporate ladder the quickest. Fortunately for me, my self-esteem was beginning to build. As I began to get new opportunities in the bank, and accolades of my own, I began to feel myself believe in myself more and more. Then, just when I thought life was on its way to being "out-of-this-world fantastic," the proverbial rug was pulled from under me. I found myself going through a second divorce. This sprinkled donut was feeling more like a donut hole at this point.

Thankfully, the Universe really does have our back. Suddenly, it was as if a floodgate opened. People and resources began to appear on my path that would assist me in healing those wounded parts of myself. I plunged full into a world of self-discovery, healing, and an ever-increasing level of self-love and self-acceptance resulted.

At the pool I met a man who handed me a brochure about an experiential workshop that would change my life. He saw my pain and suggested I attend the Woman Within training. I did. Around this same time, I found Louise Hay's book, *You Can Heal Your Life*. I did. I also joined Mary Kay cosmetics and through the brilliance of Mary Kay Ash's teachings, I was building my self-esteem while assisting others in building theirs. My life was truly beginning to feel so good.

One night while at a big Mary Kay function, I had a caricature drawn of myself. This would prove to be a really powerful experience. When the artist handed the drawing to me, I looked at it and was absolutely taken away by the image. It was a really beautiful drawing of me, and I looked exactly like my mother.

When I returned home, I called my mother and I said, "All these years, you have called me the sprinkled donut. I want you to know that I am a direct reflection of you. I look just like you. And, you are a sprinkled donut, too." That was a profound healing moment for our relationship.

I love that I am now able to live my life out loud. I no longer reside in the state of Michigan. I actually live in the state of Texas. Funny how that sweet little three-year-old sang the song of the yellow rose state, and I ended up living here.

I gave up my bland job of being a banker to follow my bliss of teaching, coaching, and sharing the principles that put me on my right path. Along this healing journey of 12 years, I met my soul mate, Kim, who has encouraged me from day one to step back up onto that "dining room table" and sing my song. He is my biggest fan. Through the years, he has showered me with his love, generosity, and adorned me in all of those things I had to sneak in my pocket and into my photos. In fact, he not only adorns me in the glitter, bling, and things, he is a photographer that takes photos of me in all that sparkly goodness. Yes! I live the life of a sprinkled and happy donut.

Recently, at a Heal Your Life® teachers' training, during the closing exercise, so many teachers said to me, "I admire you for living out loud." I almost came out of my skin. Gone are the days when people say things to dim my light. From that, I am encouraged to turn my light on even brighter. THAT is the beauty and the power of allowing one's inner light to shine.

Our light brings light to others.

Finally, as I prepare to leave you, I will share another great example of just how fun it is to shine. I was at lunch with another wee little three-year-old, Daniella. I am her "Tia," which is Spanish for aunt. On the table laid my wallet with my driver's license exposed. The driver's license photo was taken during my "dimmer" days. I had conservative, bland, and reddish-brown "banker" hair. (Eww).

All of a sudden, Daniella started to laugh very loudly. Her nose crinkled up as she joyfully laughed and questioned, "Tia, is that you in that silly crazy hair?"

Silly crazy hair? Yes! How awesome that *her* vision of "normal" for her "Tia" is hair bleached white and sprinkled with vibrant shades of pink and purple.

The story doesn't have to end here; it *could* continue here, with you choosing to be the star of your own show, shining brightly and living loudly, too!

Go ahead ... let it shine ... I promise you ... the neighbors are *not* looking. They never were.

This story is dedicated to my beautiful mother, Dolores. My hope is that in sharing this story, others will be inspired to heal old hurts and live out loud – especially mothers and daughters. I love you, Mom.

I wish to say thank you to every single experience which I mentioned in this story and to every one of them which I did not mention in this story. Had it not been for my experiences, I would not be who I am today. Thank you to my entire family: grandmothers, grandfathers, mom, dad, step-parents, sister, brother, nieces, nephews, and to those who are considered family. I am eternally grateful to my wonderful Kim. His depth of love and support is immeasurable. In this moment, I am especially grateful for the precious wee ones in my life who constantly show me by their shining examples how to be a sprinkled donut: Avriana, Bodhi, Chloe, Daniella, Gabriella, Isabella, Joaquin, Liam, Lucy, Mark, Melaney Starfish, Tijmen, and Xandria. And, to little Pete, who left us far too early. All my love!

~ Sandra Filer

Kailah Eglington

KAILAH EGLINGTON is a motivational speaker, coach, mentor and author, who, through sharing her own personal experiences, helps empower individuals to transform their lives and become the people they want to be. Founder of Life Seeds, she teaches how positive thinking, forgiveness, gratitude, and reconnecting to our inner wisdom can help individuals overcome physical, emotional and spiritual adversity.

She resides in England with her husband and two cats, where she enjoys writing, quilting and helping others discover the deep power within us that can achieve amazing things.

ke@lifeseeds.co.uk
www.kailaheglington.com
www.lifeseeds.co.uk

The Mirror

I looked in the mirror one morning and staring back at me was a stranger, a tired face I did not remember. The jaw line was beginning to slacken, the eyes were slightly sunken, the lips pursed as if in disapproval. I wondered who on earth she was – this unwelcome woman who insisted on invading my mirror.

She gazed at me as intently as I was studying her. In a parody of mime, we moved our heads from side to side, lifted our chins, and moved our fingers around our cheeks. I really wasn't amused by this at all, so I accused her of having sagging skin on her neck. Her only reaction was to inspect mine more intently. I could see that the jowls on her chin were beginning to show and that her eyelids had fallen, and I told her so. She mocked me as she pulled back the skin on her chin in an imitation of a face lift.

Spinning this way and that, like Siamese twins, hands on hips, I said: "Look at that bum of yours – you could be an ad for orange peel and for heaven's sake, pull in your stomach!" She tried vainly to tuck everything in, but ended up looking like a rag doll sitting on a broomstick. I laughed hysterically on the inside but the face staring back at me was tinged with disappointment and regret.

Not only had this silent partner taken up residence in my mirror, but she had cluttered up my bathroom with every face cream, body moisturizer, eyelid lifter and wrinkle-relaxer known to mankind! I accused her of not being a kid anymore and for believing that she could turn back the hands of time simply by using collagen in a can. I scolded her for believing the claims of eternal youth she so avidly consumed from magazines and the Internet.

The stranger in the mirror looked back at me, with her dark, cow-like eyes. A single tear spilled from eyes that had watched the birth and growing older of her children. I watched the tear slide over the cheek her children had kissed and that she had gently placed against fevered foreheads. It continued its journey over the lips that had lovingly kissed away the boo boos, mended disappointments and gave encouragement. I watched as the tear fell over her chin and dropped into the hands she held clasped at her waist; the same hands that had for years tended and nurtured her family, forged a career, cleaned her house, waved good-bye and welcomed, cooked, crafted, loved, hugged and supported family, friends and strangers.

And as I watched that stranger in the mirror, a tiny ray of sunshine caught the tear in those wonderful, loving hands and made it sparkle with the rainbow colours of recognition.

I looked up slowly and deeply into the patient eyes that watched me back, and for a moment, I saw the young, vivacious girl that still lived within. "Welcome, stranger," I said. "You must be middle age. Let's walk together."

Love Yourself As You Are

 Some people, no matter how old they get, never lose their beauty – they merely move it from their faces into their hearts.

~MARTIN BUXBAUM

The thought of getting older can sometimes be frustrating. It can be an intense reminder that time stands still for no one. The lipstick or hairstyle we've worn all our lives suddenly looks wrong; we struggle to find a style that lets us feel comfortable in our skin, and yes, we may even start to feel self-conscious or even quite worthless, in spite of tangible accomplishments in our lives.

The little story illustrates how I actually felt one morning, when I suddenly realised, then accepted and embraced, that although some things had changed physically, I was still me inside and could wear my age like a badge of courage and celebrate with all and sundry that I had begun a new chapter in my life.

The reality is that what we can achieve and celebrate about ourselves is not related to age, weight, hair colour, number of wrinkles or any of the other restrictions we choose to apply. It's about that most beautiful, unique and special person that is our true, authentic and Divine self.

Growing older is a fact of life, but how we choose to grow older is down to us. We all want to look good, but when we are overly critical of how we look, we can sometimes end up obsessing about it, using up time that could be spent really nurturing ourselves or building on our past to make time to do what it is we truly want to do.

Beauty comes from within and will glow like an eternal flame if you accept that your external covering is just a vessel in which you carry your most precious assets – your inner light and wisdom.

Say Goodbye To The Expectations Of Others

🌀 The key to successful aging is to pay as little attention to it as possible.

~ JUDITH REGAN

Everyone wants to look the best that they can, but it's important that we don't confuse this with trying to change ourselves to be in line with someone else's vision of how we should look. Physical beauty does not necessarily equate to spiritual or inner beauty. Just look at the painting of Mona Lisa. Although not considered an overtly beautiful woman, she is extraordinarily beautiful nonetheless because her inner serenity shines through the physical plane. History has also shown us that someone who is extremely pleasing to look at can have the most ugly of temperaments because they have not nourished their inner self.

One of my greatest achievements in this journey was learning to ignore the expectations of others, and it was so liberating. I started going pear-shaped following an early menopause and I became obsessed with dieting. I spent a lot of time and money in trying to become the person strangers were telling me I should become. I was glued to the numerous ads about how I would look better and feel better about myself if I signed up for this programme or that website forum. But dozens and dozens of diets and forums later, I didn't look or feel better. In fact, I felt worse about myself because I wasn't achieving their goals, and the lack of proper nutrition made me feel lethargic and unwell. That critical little voice inside my head kept saying I was a failure, but eventually I had the sense to get off that carousel and realise that my true light shone from the inside out and that I was, in fact, a sexy, curvaceous 57¾-year old woman with a nurturing and giving heart, and THAT is what people saw. In focusing on the spiritual rather than the physical plane, we allow our true selves to shine through to ourselves and to others.

That is not to say that you should not colour your hair, have plastic surgery or any other physical changing treatments; just be sure that the decisions to do so are YOURS and not those of someone else telling you what you SHOULD do.

Be true to yourself. Be comfortable with yourself. Be authentic. You are unique – there is only one of you, so celebrate it and stand out in the crowd! If we all looked exactly the same, what a dull and boring world this would be, don't you think? What I love most about life is the diversity of it; there is diversity in nature, in people, in music, food, books – in absolutely everything including you! Dare to be who you really are with love and confidence and what a wonderful gift you will give to the rest of us!

Affirmation:

I am beautiful inside and out. My inner light radiates confidence and acceptance. I am surrounded by people who love and respect me. I celebrate my uniqueness. I am complete.

Ditch The What Ifs & Rekindle Your Dreams

🦋 It is possible at any age to discover a lifelong desire you never knew you had.

~ ROBERT BRAULT

Who says it's too late to follow your dreams? Who says that just because you have a few years under your belt, you can't try something completely new or off-the-wall? Do you know that my grandmother got her pilot's licence when she was 63? That's right. She had always wanted to fly an airplane, and one day she just decided she was going to do it in spite of being told she didn't have a hope of doing so. She was true to herself, followed her heart's desire and had a whale of a time in the process.

One of the big misconceptions we have is that the older we get, the more impossible it is to learn new things. But it's not the ability to learn that we lose, but rather the confidence in our ability to learn. And how many of us have not gone through regular visits to the land of "what ifs?" What if I had gotten that degree? What if I had opened up that bakery? What if I had displayed my paintings?

It is so easy to beat ourselves up for things that have already come and gone. Could I have done something to prevent this or that? Might my life have been different if I had done this or that? The reality is that we will never know. That part of your life is gone, you have no control over it and living in the past won't change anything. What you do have control over though, is what happens NOW.

For me, I had always wanted a degree and spent plenty of "what ifs" thinking of how different life would have been had I had one. I finally decided to get off my backside and find out, but my reasons for doing so had changed. This time rather than wanting to get a degree because others thought I should have one, I decided to get one for ME. I earned my first degree when I was 55, am due to complete my PhD at 59 and to be ordained at the age of 60. And what a thrilling ride it has been and will continue to be! In parallel, I have earned a number of other qualifications and have started a new business doing exactly what I want to do and following my true path.

Affirmation:

I am open to the endless opportunities that are available to me. I am surrounded by situations and people that help me realise my potential. I am confident and excited about fulfilling my deepest desires. I am safe. I am complete.

Finding Your True Path

🌾 Nobody grows old merely by living a number of years. We grow old by deserting our ideals. Years may wrinkle the skin, but to give up enthusiasm wrinkles the soul.

~ SAMUEL ULLMAN

Sometimes we get caught in a trap of not moving forward because of fear, lack of confidence, or we don't know what it is we want to do. Do you know that one of the top search phrases on the Internet is "what is my life path?"

It's not surprising as by the time we reach middle age, many of us will have had a lifetime of raising families, working, volunteering, and looking after our elderly parents, our homes and so much more. Women especially are minefields of energy raising children, looking after the family and maintaining a home. Many of us will have had to work as well to make ends meet; many will have been single mums. Women have a legacy of multi-tasking, juggling money and time and looking after others but also have a legacy of not looking after themselves. Similarly men have traditionally been the main breadwinners;

looking after the practicalities of the home, but again very few men will sit back and look after themselves.

We rush, rush, rush around getting on with our lives and eventually forget our deepest desires. We forget to listen to ourselves, we lose connection to our inner wisdom, and we lose the serenity that each of us needs. When that happens, it's time to stop, be still and take stock or we will simply dry up inside.

 When it comes to staying young, a mind-lift beats a face-lift any day.

~ MARTY BUCELLA

So how can you be still in a world that is running wild? Well, it does take practice, but it is worth it from a physical, mental and spiritual perspective. So let's start now. Find a place that is quiet. For me, I go to the forest, but it could be your back garden, a room in your home, anywhere you feel safe. Make yourself comfortable. You can sit, lie down – whatever works for you.

Now close your eyes and take a deep breath in. Hold it for a second then release it slowly. Very, very slowly. Take another breath in and release it. Just concentrate on your breathing and nothing else. In and out. In and out. Feel yourself relax. Doesn't it feel good? Let yourself go. If a distracting thought comes into your head, imagine your finger and thumb flicking it out of your mind. Just relax and follow your breath.

When you feel relaxed, ask yourself one question: What is my deepest desire?

Imagine that your deepest desire has already evolved. See your vision now, in the present. See yourself doing exactly the thing you want to do. Feel your feet walking your life path. Is it the floor of your new shop? Is it sand, or is it walking into the cockpit of a plane? Feel it. Breathe it. Radiate it. Savour it. Feel the happiness it brings you. Feel the rewards it brings you. Hold those feelings that achieving your deepest desire bring to you then slowly open your eyes and reawaken to your surroundings. Write down what you feel, letting the pen free write your thoughts.

The next step is to strengthen your vision with positive affirmations, statements or thoughts that will help you create your best life. BELIEVE that your vision has *already happened*. BELIEVE that you are *already reaping the rewards* and *feeling the happiness* and *excitement* achieving your dream brings to you. Make affirmations the elixir of your life. The more you affirm the positive, the more good things will come into your life. Don't overthink your affirmations just keep them positive and in the present.

For me, my deepest desire was to be an author and to help others through my writing. I used to affirm that one day I was *going to be* a successful author. Although I wrote smaller articles, I still had not published anything until I changed my affirmation to "*I am a successful author.*" The result? I am now a published and successful author! Do you see the difference in the affirmations? In my first statement, I was affirming "*going to be.*" It was always in the future so was never going to happen until I placed it in the present, saying "*I am*" and believed it had already happened.

Affirmations are like learning to ride a bike. You may falter at first, but the more you say them and the more you believe them, the more they will become second nature to you and will allow you to create the life that you want to have. Saying them out loud or in a mirror makes them even more powerful and will allow you to achieve your deepest desires.

Most of all, though, you have to believe in yourself! Know that you have the power within you to create whatever life you want at whatever age you want! There are no limits.

Affirmation:

I am living my dream. I am successful with all that I do. I am surrounded by unlimited joy, abundance and love. I am complete.

Rediscover Your Inner Child

🎐 Growing old is mandatory; growing up is optional.

~ CHILI DAVIS

Another misconception we have is that we have to grow older gracefully – a concept that I refute outright!

When we are born, we are pure; our heart, our thoughts, our love is pure. We express our feelings freely; we love ourselves, our bodies and others unconditionally. We do not judge, criticise, discriminate or compare. We laugh, cry, and are in awe of every new discovery. We simply *are,* and we are beautiful.

It is so important to continue to nurture our inner child and keep alive the part of us that is still in awe of every new discovery, that can laugh or cry unashamedly and can just have fun! Who said we have to become boring old farts once we pass a certain age?

There *are* no rules to aging. If we want to talk to squirrels, sing, dance, run barefoot down a beach, roll down a hill, be silly or learn to roller blade at the age of 70, then who is stopping us? Who said there is an age limit for play?

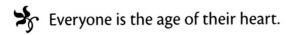 Everyone is the age of their heart.

~ GUATEMALAN PROVERB

We don't have to be childish, but we can have a child's heart and celebrate the spirit of the child within by letting our inner child come out to play more often. Simple play and laughter are important to feeling good about ourselves as we age and these feed our spiritual and emotional selves. They keep us young and vibrant from the inside out.

So, what age is your heart going to be today? Your homework is to do something silly! Jump in a puddle! Bury yourself in leaves! Roll down a hill! Make a mud pie! Tell a silly joke! Do something like this every day. But most of all laugh, love and enjoy life; it is the greatest gift we will ever be given!

Affirmation:

I am a child of the Universe filled with pure Love and Light. I am spontaneous and creative and I release the need to limit myself in any way. I am surrounded by nurturing and loving relationships. I am complete.

Grow old with me! The best is yet to be.

~ROBERT BROWNING

The stranger in the mirror melted away and in her place was me. Authentic, beautiful me stepping into my best life.

Step into yours.

All is well.

Dedicated to anyone who thinks they are past their sell-by date. Your life is only just beginning!

Thank you to Mike for his unwavering belief and support in me. To my dearest friend, Janet – may we grow old together ungracefully! To Juliet – thank you for lighting up my journey with your incredible warmth and wisdom. To my growing family of devoted readers and followers, my gratitude and appreciation of you is boundless. And to Nancy and Lisa – thank you for helping my dreams come true.

~ Kailah Eglington

Shellie Couch

Photo Credit: Deb Hagen Photography and Digital Art

SHELLIE COUCH is creator and owner of Practice Living Joy, where she provides group and individual coaching and workshops in living with joy in the present moment. She is often called upon as a speaker on the topics of the power of joy and overcoming personal obstacles.

She resides in rural Inman, Kansas with her husband. She enjoys spending time with her three adult children and her two grandchildren. She also enjoys travel and time with friends and enjoys them even more when the two can be combined.

shellie.couch@practicelivingjoy.com
www.PracticeLivingJoy.com

Pack Your Bags

When I first agreed to write a section for this book I was so excited. What a wonderful opportunity! Then I began contemplating what I was going to write about. I thought about the title of the book, *Step into Your Best Life*. Excitement began to become trepidation. Trepidation became full out fear. Fear lead to feelings of unworthiness. The stream of negative self talk turned into a raging river. "Who are you to think you can guide someone into stepping into their best life? What credentials do you have? What makes you think you are so important?" Those were only some of the thoughts running through my head.

I know that I am not the only person that has these types of thoughts. I am guessing that you have similar thoughts about things that you have agreed to do, or things that you'd like to do but don't agree to because of these very thoughts. You are not alone, not by any stretch of the imagination. I know because I am right there with you! Part of finding joy in my life and living the best life possible is looking those fears in the face and taming them. I have had quite the journey learning ways to do that.

I consider that this life is a journey. That isn't much of a stretch. I'm sure that you have heard life referred to as a journey before. I am going to offer my assistance as a travel guide for your journey. I hope to be a little manual that you can refer to every once in a while, when you want some ideas about what attractions to check into or how to pack for where you are planning to go. Sometimes having a little guide or manual to look at can alleviate some of those fears.

Preparing For The Trip

When you begin planning for your journey, it is good to know what kind of traveler you are. There are several kinds. Are you a planner? Do you need to have a specific destination in mind and a good map, all routed out with all of your stops planned? Are you a spontaneous traveler? Do you love to just "go with the flow" and end up with some extraordinary stories of unexpected things encountered? Neither is right or wrong, good or bad. It just helps to know yourself in this way because it may help you to pick the "attractions" that are right for you.

Many self-help books or books on finding happiness or peace start out by giving you "must do" tasks. A good example is that many people will tell you that journaling or using a gratitude journal is a must for getting started on that road to happiness. Don't get me wrong, I have had journals and gratitude journals. I actually love the idea of a gratitude journal as a starting point to your journey to happier you. But several people that I coach just aren't into this type of thing. I tell them not to do it. I am here to tell you that if you do something with dread or if you consider it a chore, it is not going to make you happier. Knowing what kind of traveler you are will help you decide if something is a good fit for you.

Set yourself up for success. Be open to trying things, even if they are outside ofyour comfort zone. Know how long you are willing to try something and give yourself an out. Many people say to try things for a month. I know myself. I have spent quite some time getting to know myself. I don't need a month to know if something resonates with me. I try new ideas or techniques for two weeks. I tell myself that if it isn't bringing me joy or peace I won't continue after those two weeks. My "out" is that if it is something that is creating the opposite of what I want (joy and peace) then it can go sooner. If I am truly miserable while trying out a new tool, I will drop it before the two weeks are up. I will not continue "trying it out" just to say that I did it for the entire two weeks.

Try leaving the door open. I try to remain open about things that I have previously tried that didn't work for me. Sometimes it wasn't the tool or process at all. It was that I wasn't ready for it yet. It didn't fit for me because I hadn't laid the proper foundation for it, but when I tried it later, it worked wonderfully.

Packing Your Bags

In case you haven't guessed, my favorite things to pack are some of my favorite tools for finding and staying in joy. My journey has had plenty of bumps in the road, numerous detours and lots of backtracking. There are things that I have learned along the way that were tools that I used for a time but have left them behind, things that I keep in the trunk to pull out in case of an emergency, and there are things that I keep in my ever present carryall. I would love to share all of these tools with you, but I only have space for my absolute favorites, so you are getting some of my best "carryall" tools!

✪ Reframing

One of the tools that I use every single day is reframing. It is also one of the first tools that I make sure that my clients have. Reframing is simply taking a situation that you are unhappy with and choosing to look at it in a different way.

One the examples I use frequently is a situation that happened in my family. My youngest son was at his friend's house and had agreed to watch his friend's little brother for a brief amount of time while his friend and his mother ran an errand. My son was about 17 at the time, and his friend's little brother was about 9. They were playing in the front yard with the boy's AirSoft guns. These are kind of like BB gun pistols that shoot a rubberized BB. Someone called the police, and when they arrived, my son was handcuffed and made to lay face down on the ground at gunpoint for a period of time.

When I would tell this story, most everyone would be upset that my son had been treated in such a manner, and would marvel that I didn't seem fazed by it. It was simply because I had already reframed it in my mind. If my son was 9, and someone saw a teenager pointing a gun at him, I would want them to call the police. I would want the police to take it seriously and get the situation under control immediately to ensure no one was in danger. I would then expect them to ask questions after the scene was safe. This is exactly what happened. Yes, I was sad that my son had to go through what I am sure was a frightening ordeal, but no one was hurt and the situation ended well.

I could have been angry that my son was treated in such a fashion, but what would I gain from that? Reframing the situation allowed me to be in a good place and allowed for me to maintain a high vibration. It also allowed me to be thankful and appreciative that if something were wrong, our city has officers that know how to deal with it fairly.

You can reframe any situation, and with practice, it becomes second nature. Anytime I experience something that brings my vibration down, I immediately look for a way to see it another way.

✂ Assigning Positive Intent

This is such a good way to raise your vibration when little annoyances bring it down. It is exactly what it sounds like. In any situation in which something annoys you, assign the "perpetrator" positive intent. This isn't to excuse their behavior, it is to make you feel better.

So you don't have to know if the reason you assign is true or not, but make it true for you.

I used to have a boss that would "throw me under the bus" any time something didn't go well. It didn't matter if I was really at fault or not, oftentimes it would be for her mistakes, but I would have the blame placed on me. I was the scapegoat. I was in the process of finding other employment, but needed to keep this job until I found a suitable replacement. I knew that I needed to have a way to remain thankful for my job so that another one would find me, but was finding it more and more difficult to do, until I found this little jewel.

I would make up reasons that she had to assign others (me) blame which assigned a positive intention to her. For instance, she is doing this because she is afraid of losing her job and wants nothing more than to be able to feed her family.

This didn't excuse her behavior, it didn't make her behavior right, but because I could then have compassion for her, instead of anger, it allowed me to feel better about the situation. This didn't have to be true for her; it just needed to be true for me.

Try this technique the next time someone cuts you off in traffic. Imagine that they are rushing home because their child called them in a panic, and the driver is simply trying to get home to comfort a child. It may be the furthest thing from the driver's reality, but if it is true in your reality, you are able to feel compassion and kindness for this person instead of anger and resentment. Compassion and kindness are a much higher vibration than anger and resentment.

❦ Open Ended Questions To The Universe

This is one that I have just recently come across, but it is just such a fabulous tool that I can't imagine my life without it now! The Law of Attraction is a big part of my life, and this just fits so well with it that I am unsure why it didn't appear before me sooner. This one is fabulous because it works just as well for days that have been going smoothly, days that wondrous good has been dropped into your lap, or a day when things just seem to be going awry.

"How does it get any better than this?" has become my favorite question. It doesn't matter if I just got bad news or if I just got fabulous news, it allows the universe to show me just how it DOES get better than this!

A common hang-up for those practicing the Law of Attraction is what Mike Dooley calls the "dreaded how's." This helps with that. Instead of asking myself the question, I just allow the universe to take it on when I ask (without answering,) "What would it take to get from here to there?", and then allow the universe to show me.

My husband and I were feeling some financial strain when we were assisting two of our grown children by paying their utilities (they resided together). I began asking the universe "What would it take to be comfortable again?", and within a couple of days I received a call from our daughter saying that she and her brother were feeling financially stable enough to take on their utility bills. It was a bit unexpected because from our perspective neither of our children's situations had changed, but apparently, their feelings about their situation had changed.

I am excited to see what other wonderful things happen as I continue playing with this tool. I can only imagine the wonders that are coming my way!

☙ Detaching From The Outcome

I have often found that, in my past, I would allow the outcome of something to determine my outlook on the day, or even my life, for days at a time. I have a fairly vivid imagination, and I would plan something and have a very specific outcome in mind. When things didn't go my way, exactly the way I had envisioned it, I was miserable. My poor husband has been on the receiving end of that more times than I care to admit. I would plan a picnic or a date and expect certain things to happen a certain way, and when they didn't go as planned, I would sulk and pout and feel sorry for myself, until I learned this trick.

When I plan something now, I still have a very vivid imagination and see things going a certain way, but instead of being invested in the outcome that I envision, I hold the feeling that that outcome would bring. Things don't have to go the way I envisioned them, and often-times, they go much better. I get the feeling I was going for so I am thrilled.

One of the things that help me to let go of the outcome is this little phrase, "If not this, then something better." I love that. When something doesn't have the outcome I wanted, saying this helps me to remember that the universe had something better than my imagination could conceive in store for me, and it is just around the corner. Yes, that little feeling of disappointment is still there, and I honor it and let it pass. Then I am able to focus on the feeling of wonderful and grateful anticipation for what is to come instead of wallowing in the disappointment for days.

Now that you have these four fabulous tools in your bags, we are about to begin that journey and step past all of those fears. Make sure you have a good variety of things in your bag. Wisdom from all the people you admire, wisdom from your family, wisdom from YOU! Remember to pack "lightly." Everything that is right and true for you will feel light. Things that aren't true or right for you will feel heavy. Leave all that heavy stuff behind. Remember to leave some room for souvenirs – wisdom that you find along the way.

Stepping Out To Start Your Journey

It doesn't matter if you are a traveler with a route all mapped out or are an adventurous traveler; you have to be present in the moment to enjoy it. The journey is truly not about the destination, it is about the fun, beauty, joy and lessons along the way. So set your intention to find those things. Watch for the road signs and billboards. If the same thing is being presented to you again and again, you probably need to make a detour and see that darn attraction!

I am reminded of traveling down I-70 in Kansas. There are multiple signs for Pioneer Village in Minden, Nebraska. You see them over and over again. Now, Pioneer Village isn't on I-70, as a matter of fact, at one of the shortest points it is 132 miles north of I-70, but because we had passed those signs so many times, eventually my husband and I made the trip to see Pioneer Village. We even took my husband's parents there on another trip because we knew that my father-in-law would love it. If we had never gone, we would have never had that wonderful trip with my in-laws. My husband's dad is gone now, and that trip is a memory that we cherish.

This is how many of the teachings that have meant the most to me have come to me. They will keep popping up until I finally take the bait and dive in. The things you need to have will find you, if only you keep your eyes open and take the bait.

Many people are so focused on their destination that they forget that getting there is half the fun. Be adventurous. Take some chances. Sometimes the detours that we take can shape our lives in the most fabulous ways.

Admit it, when you are driving down the highway and you see the orange construction signs, especially the detour signs, you sulk and pout for a minute or two. Me too! It is only natural. But I am here to tell you that those can be the most fabulous things in the world! Take the detour! You never know what you might find.

We have all had detours in our lives. My biggest detour was getting pregnant in high school and finding out about it right after I had broken up with the father. I had plans that would be forever changed. I had options that would have allowed me to stay on course, to keep my eyes on my destination. I chose, instead, to take the detour.

I have no idea if staying on course would have resulted in life as I had planned, but I know that the life I had planned wouldn't compare to my life as I know it now.

I met my wonderful husband as a result of that detour. He is the kindest, most generous man I know. I have the most beautiful daughter and two if the most handsome sons as a result of that detour. I have been blessed immensely because I was able to let go of the destination, the outcome that I had planned.

I know that you must have those detours, too. When you run into a detour while you are traveling along, a lost job, a transfer, whatever it is, think back to that detour that you've already encountered that worked out well for you, then jump into the detour with both feet. Jump in with enthusiasm and grateful anticipation of the wonderful things that the universe has in store for you. Remember that fear and excitement are almost identical biologically, and know that fear, with a couple of deep breaths, is nothing more than being excited. Embrace that excitement!

Don't freak out if you backtrack a bit along the way. Sometimes a lesson is just so important we get to learn it twice, or even three or four times! Actually, I have found, when looking back, that sometimes when the same situation arises time and time again, it isn't that I haven't learned the lesson from it, oftentimes there are multiple things that I have learned from it, but if the situation hadn't repeated, I might have missed one of those additional lessons.

A situation that I had to endure several times to get all of the lessons that I needed from it comes to mind. I have had several occasions in which a member of the opposite sex has propositioned me, knowing that I am happily married, one even going so far as to send inappropriate pictures to me. I would lament to my friend, wondering what I was doing wrong that I was calling this into my life. What was I gaining from this, and why did it keep happening?

I didn't tell my husband about the first time. I thought I had taken care of the situation, and there was no need to bother him. The next time it happened, I thought that the lesson was that I needed to have more trust in my husband's ability to cope with the situation, so I told him after I had taken care of the problem. The next time it happened, I told my husband before I took care of the problem, then took care of it thinking surely I have gotten what I need from this and it won't happen again. The next time that it happened, it was a non-issue for me, there wasn't a lot of thought in it. I just stood my ground and was confident in who I was and didn't realize that it had even occurred until someone pointed it out to me. I think I finally got it. There were numerous lessons, and I needed them all. I learned to be open enough to trust my husband with the tough stuff, to do it right away and I learned that if I am confident in who I am and stay true to that, then even the issues aren't really issues.

So, detours and backtracking are okay. Have fun with it. It is just part of the ride.

Finding Your Destination

Finding your destination is a tough one. I haven't done that yet. I am still on my journey, as are you. But I know this: When you arrive at your destination, if you have learned to enjoy every minute of the journey and appreciate the wondrous beauty that abounds around you, you will arrive happy. I know that the journey is about adventures, detours, and loving the people that surround you.

Knowing all of that has made it easier to step past any fear that I may have to enjoy the adventures that come my way, like writing this section for this book. Did it change the fact that I don't have any "credentials" for doing it? No. Did I let that stop me? No. I stood true in the person that I have become, the person that I am still becoming, in all the lessons I have learned on the road that I have traveled. I wrote it, knowing that someone out there is starting off where I started off, and they can benefit from the knowledge I have gained along the way.

Pleasant travels and bon voyage, my friend, as you step into your best life. I know that if you have packed your bags with the proper tools, you will have a safe and enjoyable journey!

Dedicated to all of the searchers and seekers of their best lives, and to all of those who have allowed me to be and continue to allow me to be a searcher and seeker.

I would like to thank the marvelous and magical universe for bringing incredibly wonderful people and opportunities into my life, Lisa Hardwick and Nancy Newman for continuing to have faith in me, and my family who unfailingly supports me.

~ Shellie Couch

There is no one
giant step that
does it. It's a lot of
little steps.

~ PETER A. COHEN

Nicole Stevenson

Photo Credit: Christy D. Swanberg Photography

NICOLE STEVENSON is a licensed Heal Your Life® Teacher/Workshop Facilitator, Numerologist, Level 3 Reconnective Healing Practitioner, author, speaker and overall lover of life. She is uniquely qualified to assist others transcend limiting beliefs, discover their numerical destiny and heal on all levels including spiritual, physical, emotional and mental.

Nicole lives in Calgary, Alberta, Canada where she loves to spend time with her family and friends. She especially enjoys spending time at the family cabin, reading and travelling to Maui whenever she can.

TheSereneSage@gmail.com
www.TheSereneSage.ca

Discover Your Infinite Self

I wasn't always a spiritual person, a seeker of truths or a person committed to being of positive service to others. Thankfully, the Universe has a plan or a mission for me ... this I truly believe now.

In my early 30's, I earned close to a six-figure salary working for a reputable Oil and Gas company and running my own department. To most, I appeared successful and on the top of my game. A husband, a daughter, a beautiful home, two expensive vehicles, a travel trailer, quads, a motor boat and a very promising career, and yet I was unfulfilled. Why?

I had listened to what society told me success was and how to achieve it. I had followed all the rules. Why then was I so disappointed in what I had created and accomplished? It was a vicious cycle: the harder I worked, the more money I earned, the more toys I purchased and the more miserable I became. Something was missing but what was it?

The answer was meaning. Did any of my material possessions or my perceived stature mean anything to me? Did my fancy title or my fancy pay cheque give me meaning? Did the material possessions I had acquired make me happy? When asking myself these questions, the answer was always a resounding NO! When searching deep, the only thing I could attach any true value and meaning to was my husband and daughter who I love dearly and am thankful for each and every day. Their unwavering support has allowed me to find my truths and truly live them.

Wondering where I had gone wrong, I began to contemplate what was important to me, what gave me the drive to get up every morning, what actually gave meaning to my life? If the life I had created and the person I had become wasn't giving me meaning, then what did I truly want from my life, and who was the real me? It was at this monumental point when my life took a completely different direction, a giant quantum leap down an unknown path. It was in my contemplation that I realized I needed to embark on a mission to find meaning ... to find my true self ... my infinite self! The self that knew its purpose, that loved itself and others unconditionally, that helped others find their infinite selves and lived a life full of meaning.

I started by reading everything I could get my hands on in terms of self discovery, spirituality and personal success. As I read I grew, and as I grew I obtained clarity ... clarity on what had now become my reality, my purpose, my meaning. What truly amazed me was that I had come full circle to when I was a young child.

To give you a little history, there were two things I wanted to do "when I grew up" ... to be a Solid Gold dancer and to help people. Now we all know that the Solid Gold TV show has been off the air for several years so that particular dream is impossible to achieve; and to be honest, I'm not entirely convinced I would still hold such importance to that dream.

Regardless, what an amazing discovery to realize that all I wanted to do, and all I have ever wanted to do, was to help people in any way I could. This has always been a common thread in my life; however, my assistance to those I was trying to help somehow ended up being at my expense. I was the protector of the weak, unpopular, mistreated and dysfunctional. I protected them in a myriad of differing ways from physical aggression to enabling, and yet in my attempts to save them, I was losing myself. Despite my efforts, somewhere along the way society's expectations had blurred my vision, and the only people I was helping were the tycoons I was making rich.

In my quest for the answers, I met some of the most inspirational people I had ever met in my life. Included were a Quantum Numerologist, a Reconnective Healing Practitioner, ironically enough a Hair Dresser, and a Belief Repatterning Practitioner. I now had opened Pandora's Box in terms of all the information that had just been made available to me. All of the wisdom that these women had discovered on their own journeys was now being imparted on me. Each one of these amazing inspirational women added, like puzzle pieces, their own unique vantage point and experiences which were helping me in creating my new vision. They were quite willing to share their insights and much like a sponge I was equally eager to learn.

In fact each one of them taught me something in their own unique way. The Numerologist finally provided the answers surrounding my insatiable appetite for numbers; the Hair Dresser made me realize that work shouldn't feel like work ... it should be something that you feel passionate about doing, and the pay cheques are merely the "cherry on top"; the Belief Repatterning Practitioner ... well, she taught me that the affirmations and thoughts I choose to make lay the foundation of what I am co-creating every moment of my life; and finally the Reconnective Healing Practitioner introduced me to a means to remember why I am drawn to be of service to others and one of the many avenues for that assistance.

These inspirational women helped me to envision the person that I wanted to become and to some extent, the person I had always been. In a way, I carry a little bit of each one of them with me every day. Just in case these women don't already realize the positive impact they have made in my life, and you know who you are ... Thank You ... for everything!

I would eventually discover, through a Dr. Wayne Dyer motion picture called, "The Shift," that I had reached the afternoon of my life. I was, in fact, shifting my life to that of meaning and purpose rather than of wealth and accumulation. Everything I had previously accomplished and achieved had suddenly become an untruth ... a lie. As Lao Tzu teaches in the Tao Te Ching, the land of 10,000 things had become unimportant to me, and I had discovered a reality which held no importance to accumulation of material possessions. These possessions and accomplishments no longer defined who I was or who I wanted to be, and I found myself craving a shift to a higher consciousness and awareness. It was time to find my infinite self and the dharma I was meant to fulfill.

Now that I had arrived at the first destination of realization in my new itinerary of life, I had so many unanswered questions, so many concerns and fears, and so many approaching unknowns. Yet as I endeavored to reach each of these new found truths, I arrived at a place of inspiration and eagerness instead of fear and insecurity.

Now don't get me wrong, this wasn't an overnight epiphany, but a two-year journey of self discovery ... one that continues this very day. I'd also like to point out, that in no way, shape or form, do I not have fearful emotions because I do. It's just with this new level of awareness, I try to remember to feel the fear and do it anyway. I now know that when I encounter situations where fear or resistance is rising in my soul, I have just discovered a new treasure that I have the opportunity to dissect, resolve and rise above.

Now in my mid-30's, after many books, lectures, and meditations, I've attained a new level of awareness. An awareness that includes the belief and knowing that I am the co-creator of my life, I am absolute divinity at its best, and I am that which I choose to manifest. I began to erase the societal definitions of myself that I had clung to for most of my life and was remembering who I really am. I was remembering my Infinite Self.

I am now fully aware of the nature of what it is that I can do to help people in my own unique and self-preserving way. I've found a suite of modalities and offerings in which I am able to not only offer a new frequency of healing but alignment with true life purpose and self love. A shift in a manner which speaks your highest truth and aligns you with your soul's passions.

For most, this journey naturally occurs over a long period of time and can be a lifelong shift to truth and happiness with an estimated arrival of somewhere closer to the end of your life here. However, with this unique set of offerings I am able to help those individuals speed up this evolutionary process, to help them arrive at their first destination of realization in their new and impending itinerary of life, such as I have, but much sooner.

As part of my wondrous shift to living my truth, I've incorporated my own business and am in complete awe of the incredible transformations I've witnessed thus far. I am truly blessed to be a part of the butterfly process of so many wonderful people. I like to think that each person that I interact with is not only benefiting from their experience with me but I am also benefiting from my experience with them ... it's a co-creative process in which the highest good for all is realized.

This journey has been, aside from giving life to my extraordinary daughter, the most profound accomplishment of my entire life. I've chosen to share my story in this manner in service to you and to hopefully act as an inspiration for your own evolutionary process. I encourage you to take a look at your life as you currently know it. If, you too, arrive at a place of dis-ease or discontent, such as I did, go back to your childhood, the place and time before societal norms convinced you who you should be, and not only remember who you *really* are but who you *really* want to become. Know you are not alone; know that you, too, are the co-creator of your life, absolute divinity at its best and anything that you wish to make manifest.

We are all significant pieces of the grandest puzzle, creative strokes of the most beautiful painting and inspirational leaders of our wondrous world. As you expand your abundant and creative vision for your life, so, too, does the Universe. As you discover your own Infinite Self, do whatever it takes, and leave no stone uncovered as you evolve into the highest version of yourself. Start by transcending the ordinary outer version of your Self and aligning fully with the extraordinary inner version of your Self. Don't listen to what others say is the right thing to do ... go deep inside and listen to that which is one with Source.

The transition from the ordinary to the extraordinary may not occur overnight, nor will it come without its challenges, but I assure you that you will live a life of true fulfillment and zero regrets. I myself haven't yet fully transitioned; however, I have committed to take guided steps towards the time and place where I'm able to share my innate abilities and insights with others on a full-time basis.

As you become more aligned with the highest version of your infinite self, the person you were born to be, the Universe sets in motion all the resources you will require whether you're aware of it or not. I personally don't do a lot of expensive marketing or advertising, yet the Universe, through perfect synchronicities, sends me the perfect people for both their healing and mine.

I encourage you to trust your inner guidance system by embarking on an expedition of self empowered realizations, discovering your infinite self and allowing yourself the freedom to step into your best life.

For me, in addition to my newfound calling and business, I, too, have endeavored on a journey to learn as much as I possibly can by adopting the belief that I am a student of life. Each day is a blessing and an opportunity to continue on my journey welcoming all that is arriving, taking in as much as possible and growing ever closer to Who I Truly Am. I live each day in gratitude of the Universe and its magnificent orchestra of events. I hope you will too!!!!

Dedicated to all of those who are seeking their infinite selves – may you live a life of happiness and authenticity.

Thank you to Angie, Vicky, Tania, Carrie and Leah for your supportive guidance and wisdom. Each of you inspired my evolution in your own unique way and for that I am eternally grateful. Thanks to Louise Hay and Wayne Dyer for paving the way for myself and others to live a life filled with all the wonder we wish to create. Last but certainly not least, thank you to my husband and daughter for supporting me on this path and allowing me to find my happiness again.

~ Nicole Stevenson

Don't carry mistakes
around with you.
Instead place them
under your feet
and use them as
stepping stones to
rise above them.

~ RYAN FERRARAS

Tracey Willms Deane

TRACEY WILLMS DEANE is an Artist, Author, Licensed Heal Your Life® Workshop Leader, Mother, Wife, Sister, Daughter, and Friend. She has also been a Whale-swimming Guide, Registered Practitioner of Massage and Shiatsu, Flight Attendant, Lifeguard, and Swimming Instructor.

Tracey and her newly married husband (who is also her sweetheart from high school days in Canada!) live in New Zealand with her two lovely teenage Kiwi children and Silky the dog. By living more and more consciously, and with gratitude for all that is, Tracey weaves family, career, and time for her own inspiration into a life full of love, laughter, and evolution.

artinforms@xtra.co.nz
www.tuataradesignstore.com

❦ Knowing Is Not Enough:
Be Wisdom In Action

W ho am I, *really?* In the face of any circumstance, who am I *being?* Response-able or reactionary? Conscious or unconscious? Love or Fear?

Yesterday I shut down. Yesterday I knew what to do for good health, but didn't keep it up. Yesterday I knew what to do to reduce stress, but didn't do enough of it. "Later, later ... I'm too busy just now!" Yesterday I knew that anger, as a habit, wasn't good for me, but couldn't seem to get past the pattern of volcanoes erupting every time I felt let down or put down.

Feelings were a stormy sea to ride out as best I could without drowning, so I shut them down. Needs were for the selfish and the weak, so I shut them down. I was strong, independent, capable and intelligent. I could reason my way through anything. When the Inner Tutor whispered messages in my ear, I shut them down. Intuition was only ever 20/20 hindsight, guidance twisted into chastisement for not listening.

Yesterday I was run by unconscious habits. Eventually they shut me down. Today I choose. Today, in this hour, in this moment, I choose to be aware of my emotions. Energy in motion = Feelings. I respect all of my feelings; they are signposts guiding my journey. Yesterday Life was about striving for perfection. (Don't let anyone see how imperfect

I really am inside!) The race was on! To where? For what? Who knew! But, the overwhelming sense of urgency was a strong impetus for getting busier and busier and busier. Some of it I even really liked doing. But it was all about the doing – doing more, doing it better, doing it right. Quotes like, "We are human beings not human doings," set gongs ringing through me ... So I would strive harder to do better, to do right!

"Just be," says a voice. "How?" I ask. "Be peace," says a voice. "HOW?" I beg!

"You must be the change you wish to see in the world," says Mahatma Ghandi.

"Yes BUT, Bapu, wise father, no matter how hard I try, I just keep getting into situations where it's impossible to be peaceful! Please help me?" I implore.

"The weak can never forgive. Forgiveness is the attribute of the strong," says Ghandi.

"Yes BUT, I can't, I don't know HOW. It's not working!" I'm desperately seeking!

"What would love do now?" – I don't remember where I first heard that phrase, but it became a mantra, both inspiring and tormenting me: If I knew that answer, I would *BE* love by now. I would *BE* peace. I would *BE* the change I wish to see in the world! BUT, HOW?

Gradually the whispers turned to warning signs, then to sirens and flashing lights. The way I was being in the world wasn't creating for me a world I want to be in. I fully embraced the concept of creating my own reality, but my results so far were falling short of my preferred life by a long margin. My health deteriorated from fully active to barely getting around. Eventually I was diagnosed as "chronic heavy metal poisoning from environmental toxins" – of varying sources, over many years. I had gone from fully vibrant, fully functioning, solo mother, self-employed artist including heavy physical work in sculpture, with a sideline in Whale-watching, to constant physical pain, fatigue, malaise, headaches, brain fog, nausea, breathlessness, hypersensitivity, cramps, twitches, weakness, memory loss, thinking faculty loss, and more.

I was devastated. My world as I had known it came to a grinding halt. Increasing frequency and duration of Irritable Bowel Syndrome symptoms, joined with varying combinations of the symptoms of Chronic Fatigue Syndrome (also known as M.E.) and Fibromyalgia for a nasty cocktail of illness! I consulted an Environmental Toxicity expert Doctor, and heard that the treatment can be unpleasant, with a temporary increase in symptoms. I said to him, "Whatever it takes to get well, I can't go on any longer the way I am, consistently getting worse and worse. I know there is a spiritual component, too (he agreed), and I'm studying about that, but I can't get through this on my own – I've already been trying a long time! Let's go for this Chelation Treatment."

Well, the treatment binds the toxic heavy metals that have been stored in organs (including the brain) into a form that can be excreted by the body. That's the good news. The bad news is: dislodging the built-up toxins from storage, and moving them through the body to the points of excretion, creates an acute poisoning on the way past! Therefore, I got even sicker before I got better. Many days it was hard to hold on to the "bigger picture" that this was making an improvement in the long term. Faith and trust were severely tested! The chelation took three months; the recovery has taken over two years.

Also going on in my life during the years leading up to the diagnosis were two disputes. One, a dispute with my ex-husband over the educational institution our children would attend and finances for that. Our firmly held views of "what's best" did not match up and compromise seemed impossible. I tried so hard not to engage in conflict, but felt the children's best interests would not be served by me "giving in" so tried to keep open lines of communication. The conflict dragged out for three years. The second dispute was 18 months of litigation to have a contractor's insurance pay for the mistake his employee made that resulted in a situation that was going to cost tens of thousands to rectify. The bottom line was I found myself in a state of constant stress and worry for over two years.

All the while I could hear Louise L Hay's voice, "It's only a thought, and a thought can be changed. When has criticising yourself worked? Stop all criticism, NOW. Love yourself, just love yourself!" For more on this, I highly recommend Louise Hay's book, *Your Can Heal Your Life*. In some moments it was such a comfort. In the dark, painful moments, I somehow turned even that loving, supportive advice into criticism! If only I hadn't this, or if only I had done more of that, I wouldn't be in this awful, painful, predicament now.

"If only … " A most disempowering phrase as ever there was! That and "Should" were my best whips. "I should know better, I've taught stress management and healthy living!" I know this is mental/emotional/ spiritual at its fundamental base. So how come I'm not suddenly "cured" by that knowing? What am I missing?!!! How is it I'm creating a life I don't want (physical illness and continuing conflict) when I know better? How – I didn't love me!

I was still, fundamentally, a human doing. A human doing wanting to be a human being – for sure! But still, the learning and absorbed conditioning of my upbringing and society were running the show. My life was still more driven by unconscious beliefs than conscious ones. Meaning that even though I "knew better," I was acting in ways that did not serve my highest intentions. Habits and "shoulds" not only of my immediate family, friends and culture, but also of the generations of ancestors, were chugging away, automatically keeping the train on the track. Slowly killing me, but at least fulfilling their own agendas of "shoulds."

The situation got so bad that I finally admitted that the old habits were killing me. This is good incentive to choose to change, to choose a conscious life. Bit by bit, I surrendered. I surrendered doing. I surrendered thinking everything through ad nauseum. I surrendered busyness. I surrendered everything that was not for my mental/emotional/spiritual/physical wellness. I surrendered pretending everything was all right. I surrendered independence as a suit of armour.

How could I possibly surrender when I had so much to do?!!! Quite simply, I became so ill, it was all I could do to get out of bed to get my kids to school and then go back to bed again. I was simply unable to "do" what I used to do. By learning to set my sights on bare survival mode, I could get through the days. Nights were pretty darn unpleasant, but they always passed into dawn eventually. The hamster of busyness finally got off the wheel.

One of my philosophies that has served my life well goes like this: Everything happens for a reason. I might not know, see, or understand the reason immediately, but it will eventually become evident. I'm not holding all the jigsaw puzzle pieces, so I can't see the whole picture! Trusting that the Universe is unfolding perfectly might annoy me during unpleasant experiences, but it inspires me to learn from every circumstance I'm in, "good" or "bad."

I decided that since I was stuck in bed and on the couch for the foreseeable future, while my physical healing went through its necessary stages, I would invest my time and attention in my soul. I gathered inspiring books for when I had the energy to read. Listened to podcasts and web-classes of wonderful teachers from all over the world through the internet. Watched inspiring movies when I was too brain fogged to think or read. And I slept a lot! On the occasions I had enough energy to go out, I chose my activity and people to be with carefully.

My number one goal became to learn to live my life in peace. I was fully aware that it was not just the measurable levels of toxic lead, tin, mercury, silver and arsenic that were poisoning me. Invisible – but equally toxic – were the constant criticism, negative thinking, limiting beliefs, and poisonous thought loops that would play on and on while I desperately searched for the Off Button. The upset of losing my ability to be strong and active had to give way to acceptance of "what is so" in order for me to have enough strength for healing. Stress is a result of our perception of events far more than the content of the event itself. So I clearly had a major requirement to change the lenses through which I perceived each moment of my life. Those lenses are thoughts, beliefs, and judgments. The source of my distress, my stress, my unease, and my disease is within my power to change: one thought at a time, one moment at a time.

I am not the most disciplined person, and I was so brain fogged that I could barely keep up the daily food and supplements regime needed for healing. But I committed to doing what I could remember to do, as often as I had energy to do it. Learning to BE required allowing however I was, to be what it was. I learned to accept each moment as somehow perfect in the unfolding of the Universe. I could not yet consistently accept every moment all the time – still lots of resistance and judgement going on – but knowing I could only see a few pieces of the puzzle, helped open room for Trusting in the bigger picture. Bringing awareness to the present moment, that's where the "power to choose" lives. I can choose to continue as I am. I can choose to change course.

Interestingly, now that I can look back with some perspective, the key change underlying all my positive changes, has been learning what truly loving myself looks like and feels like. It took being broken down and stripped of ability to measure my self worth on achievement status to show me the true meaning of unconditional love. Since learning to find that acceptance, non-judgment, and non-attachment, I have been more able to love all the other people in my life unconditionally.

This unconditional love does not condone "bad behaviour"! It's the act of loving of the person, regardless of their behaviour. This includes saying no to being on the receiving end of "bad behaviour." And for myself, it means loving the inner me, regardless of how much I got done, or when I've made a mistake. "I approve of myself." This is the most vital key of all! Best of all, learning to love truly, has allowed true love to fill my life. All my relationships are healing: some deepening, some reconnecting, some moving on without strings attached. I choose peace. And so it is.

Today I am grateful. I am grateful even when something is pushing a button in me that Yesterday I would have labeled annoyed, hurt, even mistreated. I am grateful because I know that inside every upsetting rock is a diamond, a gift of learning and wisdom for my soul. You may have heard this saying: "The truth will set you free ... first however, it might piss you off!"

Truth and Authenticity are the keys to freedom. And sometimes it rocks the boat!

Today I take a deep breath. Pausing throughout the day to re-set my perception lenses helps me be less reactive and more responsive to life. I consciously exhale and release the tension that has unconsciously built up. I sing. Find a task that I can be mindful during. Whatever will help me get present in this moment.

Today I am real with my kids. Yesterday I was astonished by the unconscious voices of my ancestors, criticising, chastising, constantly judging – that would bound unbidden from my mouth. "Who is that speaking? It's not what I intended to say!" Gradually through inner child healing, and consciously choosing to express my own truth, living more authentically, the voice that comes out my mouth now is more often my own. Well meaning as our ancestors were, there are a lot of beliefs and conditioning that are not what I would choose for myself or my kids.

Conscious parenting. It's challenging to be tuned into what's going on under the surface in parenting interactions. Kids' behaviour can seek love in ways we disapprove of. How then to express unconditional love for our child, and not condone inappropriate behaviour, while encouraging self discipline and authenticity in each child's uniqueness? The hardest mirror to face is the unwanted behaviour of my own child. But I know that they are always showing me an aspect of myself I tend to avoid, so today I am grateful for the gift, and look into the mirror to learn what I can release or embrace that will lead to my own healing. Invariably, the unwanted behaviour dissolves when my unresolved issue is resolved.

Today I want to ask my family to do something ... my old brain habits of Yesterday spit out a "get off your butt and help with this" kind of thought. Before I open my mouth, I choose to change the tone of voice and the wording of that request. I remember that defensiveness kills communication.

Today I forgive. Yesterday I held grudges and righteousness. "How dare they treat me like that?" Today I ask: How is it I am allowing this to happen or what belief is playing out here that I was unaware of? IF who I am being is peace and love and unattached to controlling outcomes, then what are the appropriate actions/ words/ stand to take? At what point do I release the need to control the outcome in favour of being at peace? Would I rather be right or happy?

This is not to promote condoning inappropriate behaviour! Indeed, sometimes the toughest love is to stand up for ourselves and express when a person/situation is not respectful. When we love ourselves respectfully enough, we demonstrate to the world what is/isn't okay for us. The pain of anger and resentment toward people who have hurt us, no matter how justifiable, is only poisoning ourselves. It doesn't punish the perpetrator – it punishes us. Carrying it with us slowly poisons us, prevents full enjoyment of today, and erodes our health, self-confidence, relationships, and productivity. Instead, learn from past experiences and then let it go. It is possible to release old stuck emotions without getting into the emotions. Release baggage you are carrying through guided processes that allow the energy to move, and do not require you to "re-live the story" of the source of pain. Some excellent techniques for this can be found in Richard Moat's Moativational Medicine ™.

Today, I stretch and rub my arms and legs. Yesterday I knew that the energy channels flowing up and down my arms and legs would benefit from the stimulation of a vigorous rub, but I was "too busy" to stop and do it. (Study Shiatsu.) Today, I remember at least in the morning shower routine: rub up the outside of my arm and down the inside. Rub down the back of the legs and outsides of legs, and up the front and insides of legs. Stretching whenever I remember throughout the day helps too. Since I don't make it to enough yoga, Pilates, or other structured stretch classes, I just incorporate it into my daily life.

Today, I eat and drink as much real live food as I can. Yesterday I was a junk food addict and bulimic as well. I learned to feel the feelings and let them out instead of trying to smother them with food. I learned to identify my needs, to fill as much as I can myself, and to ask others for help without neediness. Trying to fill an emotional hole with food is never satisfying. Today I choose healthier versions of "treats" and make sure that my daily eating habits are healthy with room for variations as needed. I enjoy my food and am grateful for what I can eat. Gluten and dairy sensitivities naturally preclude many foods. I supplement as needed and note when I have cravings – asking myself what might be the underlying need here, then find the healthiest version to fill that as possible. Sometimes it's a food, sometimes an emotional process.

Today I am joyfully married to my sweetheart. Yesterday I was trying to make good relationships with people who were trying to love me – but it was always conditional. Unhealthy Belief: If I fit this or that role in a way that meets their needs then they will be pleased with me and reward me with attempts to meet my needs – all masquerading as love.

Today I have learned to love and accept myself authentically, which opened the space that allowed my long-lost high-school sweetheart to re-enter my life. He always did love me, thoroughly and unconditionally, although in our youth, several family patterns played out that I could not tolerate. So in my struggle to be not replaying negative patterns, I ended up defending against true love as well.

Here we are some 27 years later, having learned a lot about ourselves, relationships, love, and forgiveness. Finally able to heal the misunderstandings of the past, forgive, let go and move on together. We recently married (had a beautiful stress-free wedding!) and look forward to sharing the rest of our lives together.

Today we are not without some misunderstandings, we still have old buttons pushed, or different underlying assumptions that need to be communicated and cleared up. But by loving and respecting ourselves, we are able to share authentic love and respect with each other. Learning to trust that neither of us would hurt the other intentionally, so when something is happening that we find hurtful, we must speak up and sort through the dynamic. Stating our experiences with phrases starting with "I" rather than "You" is a great way to own our own discomfort and express what we need to clarify, rather than blaming the other and setting up defensiveness, which kills real communication. We are able to be with our differences as mirrors to see our own patterns. These mirrors are doorways through which healing is possible.

My goal from several years ago to find a healthy evolving life partner came true in the form of someone from my past. An outcome I wouldn't have expected at all. By being open to exploring the synchronicities that brought us back in touch, and staying open to love even when old buttons were pushed and healing the old hurts, today we are in love and happily married.

Today my health and strength are returning. I am doing what I love on a daily basis. More importantly I am being love on a daily basis. When I feel upset about something, I go to a quiet spot and breath deeply. Then I might do something creative to feed my soul or meditate. This tunes me back in to my Inner Tutor, authenticity, and peace in my soul.

And if you are reading this, it means I successfully created another dream come true. For years I felt called to write and be a published author of materials that would help and inspire people. Last year, at the conclusion of my Heal Your Life® Workshop Leader training in Australia, licensed by Heart Inspired Presentations, LLC, I affirmed, publicly with emotion and conviction: "I am now a published author!" And so it is.

Today I recognize the doors of opportunity that open before me and enter in, even without knowing how it will all turn out. Trusting in the Universal Perfection of All That Is – that if I have a dream, and if doors open in that direction, then even if it's a steep learning curve ahead... that's a mountain I'm happy to climb ... one step at a time.

To all who have crossed my path and told the truth, by your words or by your actions, you are my teachers. To all who seek solutions or solace, my heart cheers you on. If I can change my life, so can you! One step at a time.

Deeper than the oceans, deeper than deep space, my love and gratitude for my Danny, Taylor, and Kenza are deeper than words can say. To all my family and friends, your love, honesty, fun, and support light up my life. Thanks to all my students for our discoveries and "light bulbs." Thanks to all the inspiring authors I read, your candles shine on possibilities. Thanks to Louise L. Hay and Richard Moat for leading by example!

~ Tracey Willms Deane

I am not
discouraged,
because every
wrong attempt
discarded is another
step forward.

~ THOMAS EDISON

Diane S. Christie

DIANE S. CHRISTIE, SPHR, in 2011 was a recipient of the Governor's award for Leadership in Management for her work in establishing an agency Ergonomics Awareness Program. She is retired from government work.

Diane is now a licensed Heal Your Life® Coach and workshop leader in Olympia, Washington. She partners with people to help (re) discover their unique skills and abilities. Diane is passionate about helping others learn how to move beyond limiting beliefs, develop and take steps to create meaningful results in their lives.

Diane and her husband experience joy through worldwide travel and spiritual adventure.

info@dianeschristie.com
www.dianeschristie.com

🌿 Find Your Significance:
From Lemons To Lemonade

🌿 Sometimes when things are falling apart, they
may be actually falling into place.

~WALL PHOTOS, POSTED ON FACEBOOK

As a manager in our Human Resources (HR) Office at a government agency, one of my favorite roles was to select, train, and develop HR staff. I loved sorting out issues and coaching people on professional knowledge, legal approaches and practices. Our HR goals were consistently to understand and know how we could improve the workplace for the benefit of all staff. We helped people identify their stopping points as well as their springboards. We helped create effective solutions. Thus, the organization became stronger and more effective. My career and current work were dedicated to creating opportunities for people to be their best, at all levels of the organization. This was my purpose.

One afternoon, Joceile, the workplace accommodation specialist, stood in my office doorway. Over the years that we had worked together, she had stood in that place many times when she needed to talk immediately. This time, something was different. Her face was flushed, lips were pursed. I thought: "Okay. Wonder what's up that would create this type of response in her?" She told me about her efforts to help set workplace conditions so that a certain injured employee could return to work. There was new, conflicting information. She shared that the injured employee's supervisor was given completely wrong return-to-work information by someone outside of our office. If acted upon by the supervisor, the effect would undo Joceile's previous work, not to mention be professionally unsound and likely illegal.

The taste of sour bile was rising in my throat. I was more than annoyed. The two of us together fed off of each other for a few minutes. No solutions, we just gave voice to the frustration. The air swirled around us like at the beginning of a thunderstorm. Sound familiar to anyone?

After Joceile left, I sat alone, behind closed doors, and reflected upon our conversation. Here we were again, going around in circles. She was right to express her angst to me as her supervisor. The most important questions resulting from our conversation were: "What's the impact on our people? And impact on our organization?" I knew that unclear job accountability and awkward reporting relationships had existed for way too long, and we just worked around them. We had adjusted our work to personalities involved and to organizational structure. I had felt held hostage to circumstances. Until now. I felt "finished" with what seemed like external disregard for our employees and our HR processes in the described and similar situations.

Life is funny. Each of us has soul stirring moments. This was one of mine. Yes, if there ever was a call to concerted action, it was that moment, in the Spring of 2007, and that conversation. The next question to self was "What am I going to do about it?" I felt quite done with the status quo and feeling victimized by a situation which I had perceived as untouchable. My stomach felt like it was squeezed in a knot. Now was time to work *through* the awkwardness, decide what we really wanted to accomplish, and what our true contribution could be. Now was the time to look within. Something needed to change.

Here is the story. Center stage of the drama was, internally in the agency, how we processed and managed our worker's compensation claims. This work also included our relationship with another agency, Labor and Industries (L&I). "It" included how HR staff worked with each other, and how HR staff worked with our supervisors and managers and other employees. And at the foundation, "it" was about our injured employees. We wanted to actively manage injury claims. We wanted our employees to know they were missed and valued. We wanted them safely back in the workplace. We needed to figure out how supervisors and employees could be actively responsible for their safety. AND we needed to determine what ideas to implement and steps to take to encourage and ensure a safer and more productive work environment. Whew!

Visualize a three legged stool. One leg was workplace accommodation. Another leg was coaching supervisors on effective and legal HR approaches to managing employee job performance. These two "legs" were located in the HR Office. The third leg of the relationship – the agency process for our worker's compensation claims – reported elsewhere in our agency.

In the first place, we wanted to prevent injuries. Secondly, if injuries did occur, we needed active management of the claims. We wanted to appropriately help employees return to a safe and productive workplace. For a truly meaningful process, we needed to align our thoughts and actions.

Well, many interoffice discussions ensued about the "third leg of the stool." Ideas abounded. I, my boss and her boss, and with input from affected others, defined the work and results expected. We decided on an organizational change to consolidate all three "legs" into the HR

Office. In other words, we brought together all affected parts of "the process." We could build a solid work structure. We could streamline processes, improve communication and partner with staff more effectively. In concept, this approach seemed straightforward.

A friend of mine recently told me I was a "puzzler." She said that I loved to take pieces of a puzzle and put them together. True assessment. I love to work with people to discover underlying issues, sort out their truths, and then help create movement for more satisfying results. In this situation, I knew that safety and accident prevention was part of an integrated, holistic approach to wellness at work. That said, I was off and literally 'running' to further put pieces of this puzzle together.

Devoted time and energy was needed to focus on and help achieve our new vision and goals. After a well-planned, intense recruitment and selection process, I hired Lonnie in August, 2007. Lonnie had recently retired after a 20 year career in the US Army. He was a team player. He had personal discipline, ideas and energy. He was excited for the next chapter in his life and wanted to work, hard. He caught the vision and immersed himself in sorting out our claims.

We went on a mission to ferret out more data, analyze processes, and discover underlying attitudes. We wanted to learn how we could make a difference in shifting a work culture to focus on prevention and education, for the benefit of all staff.

Here is what we found. Our claims experience rating was shockingly bad. Yes, this is just like car insurance. The more claims, the more expensive the insurance. The more injuries at work, the more the agency and its employees pay for insurance. Most important, this was about people's safety. We found that, in 2007, my agency had the highest claims experience rating for the State for general government agencies. Our ratings were even higher than law enforcement and corrections. Ouch! Picture this ... most of our employees worked at desk jobs! How was this circumstance even possible?

Lonnie researched and analyzed the previous five years of worker's compensation claim statistics. He reviewed Occupational Safety and Health Administration (OSHA) records. He did the same with medical leave files, job description information, employee complaints and grievances, and documented requests for office ergonomic evaluations, and workplace accommodations. The work was exhaustive. Each of our update meetings contained more clues for continued research. It was almost as if we were at an archeological dig! One layer unearthed led to another.

We had such a strong desire to improve. We propelled ourselves forward. It became abundantly clear we were on the right path of research and discovery. We found a treasure trove of information and clues. Gradually the picture developed. When information was correlated, trends emerged. Actually, that's an understatement. Trends shouted out loud from the paper on which they were graphed.

Besides the data, we unearthed long established thought patterns and attitudes. Examples of limiting thoughts were: "We do not have enough money to fix your desk. Make do." Or "I do not want to make waves and ask for help." Or "That is management's problem, not mine." Or "I do not have time." And so on. As we dug deeper, it felt like we had uncovered amongst our staff a pervasive sense of despair that led to disengagement and disconnect. Most supervisors and employees wanted to do the right thing, but received consistently conflicting information. Confusion was a recipe for lethargy.

Now that we knew more, we discussed consequences of continued inaction. We talked through methods to reintroduce tools for job clarity and personal accountability. Lonnie established mutually productive relationships with the claims managers at L&I. They were excited to work with him, help him with his training. L&I staff shared ideas for internal claim management and ideas for specific actions. L&I shared their programs so we could structure our training and educate our staff. We were excited and knew benefits for all staff could abound.

Soon, Lonnie was invited to attend one of our agency's statewide managers' meetings to present and share the findings. He used PowerPoint to present charts showing our claims experience rating compared to others. He explained the financial cost of our agency's insurance premiums. He presented color-coded charts showing employee time loss from work. What we could not graph was the emotional toll on the employees and their respective work teams. Everybody was affected. All who had experienced an injury or employee time loss understood the impacts of doing demanding, time-restrictive work without enough people.

After Lonnie's presentation, and as you can imagine, his phone rang steadily. He was invited to share the compiled information to many team meetings throughout the agency. He went and he presented. Managers and employees became curious, took notice, and wanted to take action. People wanted to "fix" their work areas. In most instances, people were willing to examine some of their long-standing attitudes and misconceptions.

In October, 2008, our work took a more formal turn. Based on pages of credible data, we decided to form a working committee with the purpose of creating an ergonomics program for our agency. We had already learned that 50% of our L&I claims resulted from musculoskeletal disorders (MSD), such as muscle strain or back strain, that happened at work. This statistic was shocking and liberating at the same time. It meant that we could easily and concertedly take preventive steps which could have dramatic results. But, we had to take action to redefine "normal."

The new, core committee was made up of five people, all of whom had a vested interest in a new program, from very different perspectives. With much excitement and trepidation, Lonnie and I became members of this committee. The vision was clear. We had a mission, charter, and executive support. We would create something new, never before done in our agency. Each potential path required examination and change in fundamental thinking about how we did business, about who was responsible for what work, and how we measured our results. The only possible barrier was, as a self-directed work team, we were leaderless.

Lonnie stepped up and offered to schedule meetings. Work was assigned to each of us by all of us. We met and met. We correlated information. Our work bore fruit as we formulated the basic outline of our new ergonomics program. As more discussion and definitive action occurred, something changed. There were committee member comments such as: "But we have always done it this way." *And* "They will never go for that idea." *Or* "That idea won't work because of the history of what happened when ..." and more. As we peeled back each layer of resistance, conflict emerged and, under pressure, squirted into the open, onto the table.

Committee work became a struggle. It was one step forward, then one step backward, and then another step hardened in cement. My own experience was that of seeing fabulous opportunity, wanting to create solutions, and then being met with active resistance. There was story telling outside the meetings. There was adamant refusal to do agreed-upon work. There were constant contrary opinions about why the new work could not be done. In addition, there was ongoing admonition why our new work would never be accepted, by anyone. I felt like our committee meetings and actions sometimes resembled episodes of the TV program *Survivor*. Here we all were, on a committee with no appointed leader. Amongst us, clearly, the vision was different.

As time passed, I used my internal will to be calm and stay focused. I used attitude and leadership skills to model behaviors that I hoped could help us achieve success. There was a vision, and I persevered. Finally, there was agreement on dates, and on a basic plan. Together we created a 11" x 14" calendar encompassing *who, what, when, where, why* so all involved knew what was happening, schedules, resources needed, and expected outcomes. There was movement, yet some movement was so much more difficult than it needed to be.

Soon, our committee was scheduled to attend an Executive team meeting. More committee meetings and more disagreement occurred. I lost sleep. This was such an exciting opportunity. I wanted desperately to understand why people would *not* want to experience acceptance and success of the team's ideas. What was at stake that some people would fight so hard for the status quo? Especially since it seemed that the status quo was not working effectively for most people's benefit.

Another manager and I made the presentation to the Executive team in mid-May, 2009. The proposal and content received rave reviews. Our plan was enthusiastically accepted! As a matter of fact, some listeners wanted to begin the program even sooner than our planned Ergonomic Awareness Month scheduled for September. Wow. For some of us, it was heartwarming and downright thrilling to talk to an enthusiastic audience. Especially from the Executive team who was willing to commit resources for the benefit of the staff and the agency.

And, more meetings occurred. I felt the bittersweet sensation of knowing an excited audience awaited, yet experienced disagreement, withdrawal, and withholding within the team. I really wanted to understand what was happening. Yes, the status quo was being radically altered, and people's comfort zones were challenged. For sure, this was a call to grow, professionally and personally, for all of us. Here was an opportunity to persist and help manifest a great result for all concerned. I realized that my purpose was my anchor.

The Ergonomic Awareness Month was nearing. One beautiful and sunny Sunday morning, in July, I was at the office. I had already been there for close to five hours. There were easel sized papers taped and pinned over all four office walls. From a "distance," I was checking to ensure all the pieces were in place.

Like the proverbial bolt of lightning, an insight struck me! My assignments were on track. Lonnie's work was on track. I was willing to do most anything for the success of the project. *Now* I was doing other people's work in order for the project to be successful. I had moved beyond what was mine to do. Another Wow. At that startling realization and with some beads of perspiration on my forehead, I focused back on a document on my PC. I rewrote the last two paragraphs of a memo and affirmed agreed upon responsibilities by everyone on the team. It was time for personal accountability, for me, too.

The next day, tired, yet relieved, I told my boss of the realization and change of efforts on my part. I swallowed hard while talking, yet it was the truth. The day before and right then during the conversation, I had stepped into another aspect of life. The same lesson learned again ... each of us is responsible for results in our lives. I was afraid that our Awareness Month and all its attending communication and training intricacies might be sloppy and ineffectual. I had an abundance of mental conversation about "failure," "embarrassment," and "woe is me."

There is nothing quite as exhilarating as the experience of "letting go." I "released" others to do their best work. I "released" myself from feeling responsible for others' actions. I decided to believe that all concerned would step up to the plate and fully follow through. Guess what? Everyone did! There were some bumps, some very tense and terse conversations about agreements, but it worked. The Ergonomics Awareness Month, the training requirements and the actual training, and communications were substantial and meaningful. All staff learned about simple accident prevention, basic office ergonomics, being responsible for our own safety and how to educate others on their safety responsibilities too. Staff loved and enthusiastically accepted the education. Many stated they finally understood and had real clarity about their own responsibilities for safety at work.

Soon, fewer accidents were happening in the workplace. More ergonomically- appropriate equipment was being installed and used in the workplace. When people did experience a workplace injury, their absences from work were of shorter duration. All levels of staff were working together. We had common goals, shared energy, and consistent application of knowledge. Information previously sent only to agency executives, was now posted on the agency intranet. The data about ongoing injury and cost statistics was available to all staff. People offered to help each other. People shared their success stories. Here was our vision "come to life."

It takes some time for the cumulative effect of new knowledge and different actions to show up in ongoing attitudes of staff, cost of claims, and resultant claims experience rating. For perspective, in 2007, our cost of claims was close to $1 million per year. In 2010, claims cost decreased to about $175,000. In January, 2010, the agency's claims experience rating was 1.8849, the highest in general government and, again, not an enviable placement at all. However, in January, 2011, the experience rating had dropped to 1.4137, a reduction of 25%, the maximum allowed by law!

The story continued. In January, 2012, the claims experience rating dropped again by another 25%, again the maximum allowable. AND, insurance premiums saved for 2011 and 2012 together was over $378,000! These decreases benefitted the employees in many ways ... the lower the risk, the safer people are; the fewer injuries that occur, less money is deducted from an employee's pay.

I have my own perspective on who said what, when, and so on. *My lessons learned?* I was willing to change my belief and learn how to express that change. I focused on purpose, stayed true, and dealt with obstacles as they appeared. Holding a clear vision helped focus and refocus energy, mine and others. We all owned the result. I learned, again in my life, that stepping up to what is mine to be and do is sweet success.

I think life is like eating ripe fruit. Pretty juicy, if you're willing.

What's your perspective?

Dedicated to us All and our abilities to recognize options, choose wisely and to act.

Thank you ...

Joceile Moore, for speaking so clearly and specifically AND for being a leg of the stool

Beth Hesse, for your calm demeanor and wise approaches AND for being a leg of the stool

Jan Smallwood, for your support throughout my time at Licensing

Alan Haight, for your support of the vision, plan, and results

Lonnie Spikes Jr., for always being at work, stepping up and doing your best, consistently being willing to learn and grow AND for being a leg of the stool.

~ Diane S. Christie

Each step you
take reveals a new
horizon. You have
taken the first
step today. Now,
I challenge you to
take another.

~ DAN POYNTER

Merrill Stanton

MERRILL K. STANTON is a teacher of transformational change, a licensed Heal Your Life Coach/ Workshop Facilitator, hypnotherapist, author, and speaker with a private practice in San Diego, California. She sees clients in person or on Skype and conducts workshops throughout the world. She enjoys travelling and spending time with her daughters Hilary, Justine and son-in-law Rob in Los Angeles, California.

Merrill is also an Integrative Holistic Health Counselor. As a cancer survivor, she teaches the role of raw foods, green juices and cleanses to bring the body back to optimum health.

mkstanton@cox.net
www.merrillstanton.com

❧ I Love My Colon

A Health Opportunity

It was a beautiful sunny morning in Scottsdale, Arizona and the beginning of the week. There were so many things on my "to do" list as I was preparing to go back to Arizona State University. I decided in 2009 at 60 years old to get a bachelor's degree in health promotion, and I was nearing graduation. I loved the academic environment, the campus, the students and the teachers. However, what happened that day put in motion a cascade of events which changed the way I would live my life in the future.

In September 2010, I visited my primary doctor to ask if I could be tested for vitamin or mineral deficiencies. Even though I was eating healthy organic foods, I wanted to make sure I was getting all the vitamins I needed without taking extra supplements. The doctor advised me that insurance companies do not cover this type of test, and he offered to give me a different blood test. It was a surprise to me when I discovered I had an iron deficiency. He then prescribed iron supplements and suggested I have a colonoscopy to see if there was any internal bleeding. At least it was a start, so he said.

What If It's Cancer?

The earliest appointment available was on January 10, 2011, and I had no major concerns about the exam that would cause me anxiety. I wasn't on any medications, and the only surgery I listed was a tonsillectomy. I remember waking up from the colonoscopy procedure and hearing the doctor tell the patient in the next cubicle, "Everything is clear!" Groggily, I thought I would be next and hear the same thing.

Instead, she opened the curtain with a worried look on her face. When I asked why, she told me she discovered a large growth that was too large to remove without surgery. She said it would take a week for the pathology report to come back. I didn't know how to react except to think if I need surgery then I will manage.

However, after getting dressed, I met my husband who was waiting for me, and then I voiced my concern to him: "What if it's cancer?" He didn't believe it could be, and that helped me to keep my anxieties and fears at bay. I decided then not to tell anyone until I had a confirmed diagnosis that something was really wrong.

The next morning the phone rang early, and the doctor's name appeared on my caller ID. I knew this was not a good sign that all was well with my health since it had only been one day, not a week. She explained to me that the pathologist had contacted her right away because when he saw the biopsy, he immediately suspected it was cancerous. She told me that I should not delay the surgery. I took a deep breath and told my husband the news!

Initially, we were both shocked, and then the reality began to slowly unfold in my mind that I could actually die. Thoughts seemed to unravel quickly: There were so many things I was planning to do, and what about my two daughters, what would they do without me? The situation seemed surreal because I felt healthy and was simply looking forward to school starting the following week. My next thoughts were: Who would I tell, how would I tell them; and what should I do first, call the surgeon or the family?

As the panic began to rise, I remembered my calming method. Whenever I become panicky, I remember to slow down and breathe. I take a few deep breaths and tell myself one simple word, "relax," and then take a few more deep breaths, and as I exhale say the word "calm." It is then that I can go into a place deep inside myself that is centered and grounded. I know that in this place that no matter what is going on out there, "all is well inside." As soon as I felt calmer, I knew the first thing I needed to do was make the surgeon's appointment.

"One thing at a time" is my answer to managing the complexities of life. Somewhere I knew in my heart, mind, and soul that I was "more" than the cancer, and the cancer was a messenger. It was time to begin to review my life more closely and discern what the messages might be. I knew that if I did that and took the right actions, the cancer would go away and not return.

The next morning I was in the surgeon's office with my husband, and the doctor explained he would need to do a re-section of my colon by removing the ascending colon and 60 lymph nodes. It sounded dramatic to me, yet I agreed to schedule surgery for the following week and on the very same day school was to start!

I was so disappointed about missing the first day of school, and even more disappointed when the surgeon said I needed to withdraw from the university, at least for now, in order to recover and heal. Naively, I thought it might take a week or two to recover. A long recovery was not in my plans, and it was upsetting.

Now It's In God's Hands

I did not want to suppress my emotional responses, especially now that I was more conscious of healing on all levels, so I turned to my spirit guides for assistance in dealing with these disappointments. God loves us, and I find that these spirit guides are here to help us whenever we call on them. So, I asked them for guidance on this. I closed my eyes and felt the "whole school experience" flow through my mind, body and spirit; everything that I loved about being at school flooded my thoughts. Then I visualized walking into the building, being at the bursar's office, talking to the staff, and most importantly, feeling perfectly okay when asking to withdraw from school.

After this was complete, my perception and reaction had changed. I knew I had set in motion a different time line for graduation. When I achieved acceptance of the situation, it was freeing, and I chose to contact close friends at school and ask them for their prayers. I was joyful again as I was already thanking the Universe for the amazing experiences at ASU and all the ones in the future to come. That afternoon I withdrew from the school and was ready for the next step on this journey.

It soon became apparent to me that having a re-section was bothering me. I started to become depressed about the thought of it, and it worried me that maybe I would have complications with my digestive system. I closed my eyes again and invited in all of my guides. I was able to realize that I didn't have to look at this event as a loss, instead I could *bless* these wonderful parts of my body for the amazing job they have done all the years I have been alive.

I took a few moments and really felt the appreciation and gratitude I had for their service to me. I told them they were getting early retirement, and they would be going to a special part of heaven just for colons and lymph nodes. I imagined them as a happy little organ and nodes. I know that the little book, *Love Your Body,* by Louise Hay prepared me to love and appreciate every part of my body.

I then asked all the angels to fill the space in my body where these parts were, at the right time and in the right way, except this time *energetically,* and allow my body to function perfectly without digestive problems. I just imagined it all happening perfectly like a rain shower of energy in beautiful colors. I could see in my mind's eye everything healed with new energetic nodes and an ascending colon.

However, I did go for a second medical opinion just to be sure I wasn't too hasty having a re-section of my colon. The second doctor confirmed the surgeon's decision based on the pictures of the cancer and description in the report. Even so, I still went back and forth about this until I talked with my daughters, who convinced me that my greatest chance of survival would be the surgery. So, the decision was made. Now it was in God's hands, and I let it go.

The recovery after surgery is no picnic, you need a lot of pain medication, and you feel terribly weak. This period of recovery lasted almost four months. Now I understood why the surgeon had told me I needed to withdraw from school, he knew this would be far more complex than I realized.

What About Survival?

On February 14, 2011, I had my first appointment with the oncologist. This is the day everyone is celebrating *love,* and I was going to speak with a Doctor about poisoning my body with chemotherapy. Where is the irony in this? However, I set an intention for this meeting that I would listen to everything the oncologist said and still be able to embrace responsibility for my personal choices.

The oncologist was very nice and took extra care to explain the process and the potential side effects without trying to alarm me. However, I was not convinced and told him I was going to explore other options as well. He was very supportive and mentioned Naturopathic Specialists in Scottsdale, specifically, Dr. Daniel Rubin, who frequently worked with him while patients did their chemotherapy treatments. The oncologist then handed me a study on the drug that would be used along with a copy of the pathology report for my files. He told me I had a two-week window regarding my decision about chemotherapy for it to achieve optimal results.

Many thoughts went through my mind when I made the next appointment with Dr. Rubin. The staff was friendly, and his office was very busy with other patients taking vitamin therapy after their chemotherapy treatments. He read my pathology report and explained to me that my cancer cell was called mucinous adenocarcinoma, which means that mucous was surrounding the cancer cell. It is very rare and accounts for only 10-19% of all colon cancers and, is believed to be more aggressive because the mucous makes it easier to transport cancer cells to other parts of the body. It pays to read your pathology report because they can contain surprising information. Dr. Rubin said it could be harder to treat even with chemotherapy because the cancer cell is trapped in the mucous that protects it.

His explanation made me think about the stress in my seventeen-year marriage. I felt trapped, just like that cancer cell, in a relationship that was not nurturing me. I remembered telling myself many times over the years that the dynamics in our marriage could make me sick. Now I had cancer, and it was in my colon – an organ of elimination.

Even though my husband and I had gone to counseling and marriage workshops, we continued to struggle with the same problems: He was chronically depressed, and I was always trying to fix that. It was not a good situation for either of us, but I had buried these feelings because

I wasn't prepared to deal with the issues of leaving. I knew I would have to deal with them now for *any* treatment to be successful. I heard these messages as signs for what needed to happen inside myself if true healing were to take place.

Dr. Rubin suggested I start IV therapy with Vitamin C, and he prescribed supplements to build up my immune system. I felt this was the first step to my recovery and healing.

I continued to meditate daily, listening for an answer whether or not to do the chemotherapy. It is not easy to be in limbo, and that is how I felt up until the day before I went to see the oncologist for my follow-up visit. A few nights before my appointment, I thought about my life again and the consequences of the decision whether or not to do chemotherapy; it's a scary decision to make.

Mirror On The Wall

I decided to flip this conundrum upside down, and ask what it was about death that scared me? This was the scariest thought I could come up with, and the one I really didn't want to face. I learned a saying a long time ago that fear is an illusion and only love is real. I often use this acronym with clients, fear is *false expectations appearing real*. This thought now allowed me to look at my situation with a different perspective. I reasoned that death will happen to everyone, and no one knows when this will be. I recalled the saying that death and taxes were two things we have no control over. I don't know why these thoughts comforted me, but they did. I suppose it takes the pressure off when you realize you have no control over certain things.

There was no guarantee I was going to make the right choice. Guarantees somehow give us a sense of control, and yet, do they really exist? Even the oncologist has a document to sign, in case a patient or their family might want to take legal action in the future, indicating that he could not guarantee chemotherapy would work or the cancer would not return. It was going to be a risk either way. Once I realized this, it became much easier, and I could decide what was important to me, what the risks were and what the things were that I valued.

I began to think about the quality of life I wanted in the future whether it is was one day, one week or many years from now. When I looked at the chemotherapy treatment and its many side effects, neuropathy stood out for me as the riskiest. The doctor explained to me that it usually goes away within a period of time after the treatments ends; however, when I inquired further, there was no guarantee that it would go away.

The risk of neuropathy *lasting* was not acceptable to me. It didn't fit in with my vision for the quality of life I wanted, walking on campus, travelling the world, hiking, and enjoying a simple walk. I went through all the negative risks I would be taking with chemotherapy. When it became crystal clear to me that the approach to chemotherapy was to flood the body with a poison that attacked cancer cells *and* healthy cells, it sounded like a war.

I knew that I could not voluntarily subject my body to this attack. I could not accept doing that to healthy cells and still honor my body. My body needed a chance to build up my immune system – not compromise it further. That's what strong immune systems do, they handle diseases. Furthermore, chemotherapy treatments do not guarantee that cancer will not return, and they don't guarantee your quality of life in the future.

I believed the investment in my future was about making changes in my lifestyle. This is what all my education had been about. Now I wanted to focus on how I could change the chemistry in my body so that it wasn't a friendly environment for cancer. I knew I could enjoy learning how to change my life so I could be cancer free.

I was glad I knew it was cancer, because it took the fear out of cancer, too. Now I could embrace the concept of education, change, and transformation if I wanted to become healthy. There are many case histories of people surviving without chemotherapy. It was a *risk,* but one I would regret if I never tried. I was ready to learn. I set an intention that the discussion with the oncologist would be positive, and we would all be on good terms.

When my appointment came and I informed the oncologist of my decision not to do chemotherapy, he surprised me by saying he would be supportive and would continue to give me blood tests every three months to see how I was doing. I greatly appreciated and respected him for supporting me, and for allowing me to continue to see him for future blood tests. I then told Dr. Rubin I would follow his protocol without doing any chemotherapy.

In my research, I came across many raw food websites specifically addressing cancer. In a week's time I decided to hire a raw food health coach, Chef Sara, who had healed herself from cancer without surgery. She put me on an intensive wheat grass and green juice-cleanse for nine days and educated me about the benefits of a raw food lifestyle. When Dr. Rubin learned I was pursuing a juice cleanse, he told me about another place called Optimum Health Institute which is also known for its juice cleanses and raw food detox program.

Let Food & "Loving Yourself" Be Thy Medicine

I discovered that Optimum Health Institute offers a wonderful three-week mind, body and spirit program of healing if you want to let go of stress and give your digestive system a vacation. The guests quickly bond as we all have the same purpose to become healthier. The environment takes on a positive and loving personality all its own, and guests continue to come back year after year.

The classes are informal while giving you an opportunity to look at your lifestyle with a fresh perspective. If there are areas which need changing, they teach the tools to make those changes. I especially liked their weekly *release ceremony* which gave everyone a chance to release something from their lives that was no longer serving them to grow.

There is education about the digestive system and how the body functions better with live food nutrition. The program includes daily exercise classes, which are designed to help the body detoxify so you can eliminate toxins. It is a detox retreat center, so you do live on green juices, wheatgrass shots, sprouts, seed cheese and raw foods: Yes, it's different! There are classes that teach you how to prepare raw foods when you go home, and it's not just about making salad. The philosophy at Optimum Health Institute is that all conditions are considered a health opportunity, and this means they are an opportunity to learn and grow. This offered me a new perspective and a positive approach to take responsibility for my health.

When I came back from OHI, I had my first blood test to see if I had any markers indicating cancer: There were none! The oncologist told me everything was in the normal range, and in fact, the number for my immune system went from 2.0 to 1.6 so it was even stronger! He graciously said to me, "This is working for you, so keep doing what you are doing."

I then decided to apply to Optimum Health Institute as a volunteer for their missionary program when my three-week program ended. The missionary program is a three-month commitment which allows you to stay on the whole program, while giving the Institute 20 hours a week of service that supports their staff and guests. It was the best decision, I loved the experience, and I knew I was healing in this environment.

After the missionary program came to a close, I felt more prepared to talk with my husband about our marriage. I set an intention that the perfect occasion would arise, and the subject would come up easily and effortlessly. I did not want extra stress at this time in my life when all my efforts were to heal from cancer and reduce stress.

One day, within about two weeks of my being home, my husband and I got into a disagreement. He often said at these times, almost automatically, "Why don't we just get a divorce?" This time I answered, "Okay, let's do it." I know he was taken aback by my answer, but I knew it was the right answer for both of us, and the time had appeared easily and effortlessly just as I asked in my intention.

I understood that he was not to blame for our marriage problems, and we were both responsible for staying married if we were unhappy. I knew we still loved each other so it was a difficult choice to separate. We remain close today, and we were able to settle everything in a loving and supportive manner.

The cancer came for a reason, and it wasn't to blame anyone or any situation. It fact, my life has opened up to so many new positive opportunities. I don't believe it was genetics either. The cancer was a chance to become healthier and happier. I know my body chemistry was out of alignment or the cancer cells would not have started growing inside. I look back at the stress in my life, and how I had been handling it, and now I will change the way I handle stress in the future. I can listen more carefully and deeply to the messages the first time around, when I realize something is not right and could make me sick.

The classes at OHI and with Chef Sara taught me the importance of raw foods and enzymes. Everyone's digestive system is unique, but on this program I could feel the nutritional difference. My body needed the live food nutrition, and it's an amazing discovery to feel more energized and revitalized without meat, dairy, white sugar products and cooked foods. One of my daughters has also adapted raw foods into her life and has found the same energized feeling from green plant nutrition.

When I embraced my health, it freed me to look beyond my own limited thinking and the limited thinking around me. There is a book I would like to recommend for anyone facing cancer. It is called *Embrace Release Heal* by Leigh Fortson. This book details her personal cancer journey from traditional medical treatments to healing cancer with raw foods. It is a rich source of alternative practitioners with their contact information at the end of each chapter.

Learning To Dance In The Rain

On a deeper level, doors closed and new doors opened. As I opened to the love in the Universe, all of my relationships with family and friends deepened or healed. Before, I used to isolate myself with a sense of independence, and now I feel loved and supported in meaningful ways.

We are all masters at creating our thoughts and therein lies our greatest power. If we allow our creative minds to welcome in new thoughts which serve us to grow and be healthier, we will attract what we need to become happier. When I affirmed my willingness to be receptive to change, I released my resistance to struggle, and it was then I allowed myself to be in the flow of the Universe. The answers and treatments came to me in exactly the right order, at the right time and in the right place.

I came across a quote from an anonymous author which I think speaks beautifully to living life with true power as a free spirit: "Life isn't about waiting for the storm to pass, it's about learning how to dance in the rain."

I am cancer free today, and yet it isn't about whether my choices are your choices. It is about listening deeply and knowing that loving yourself is not just a thought but an active process that allows you to heal.

Thank you, Universe, and I LOVE MYSELF EXACTLY AS I AM.

Dedicated to supporting others facing cancer and those that support them.

A special thanks to the many authors I've learned from, teachers and mentors along the way, especially Louise Hay, Shakti Gawain, Florence Scovel Shinn, Dr. Patricia Crane, Rick Nichols, and Dr. Jack Chisum from Arizona State University. Thank you to Bill McGinnis whose support and love I deeply appreciate in my life. And thanks to all my family, friends and classmates from The Wheatley School who supported me with their prayers and words of encouragement on my cancer journey and healing.

~ Merrill Stanton

Consider the
possibility that
the little obstacles
in life are not
obstacles at all, but
stepping stones.

~ NEALE DONALD WALSCH

Deb Wright

DEB WRIGHT is participating in her second opportunity at writing a multi-author book with *Step Into Your Best Life*. After her experience with her first one, *Beautiful Seeds of Change*, the creative juices haven't stopped flowing, and her new passion has now been forever awakened.

When Deb is not writing, she spends most of her time running her business in the Philadelphia Area as a Landscape Designer while spreading her artistic mojo in drawing, photography, and, of course, writing!

justdebb@comcast.net
www.justdebb.net

🦋 Stepping Out Of The Shadows Of A Hero

Gillybean Magic

Hurry up Re, grab the popcorn and wine, our movie is about to start! Ahhhhhh, *Practical Magic*, the movie that sums up my sister, Re, and I in a nut shell. It's this cute chick flick about these two sisters, Sally and Gillian, who have this unbreakable bond, deal with the family curse, and, of course, someone is always looking for love (it wouldn't be a chick flick without that!).

Well, when it comes to me and Re, the words "unbreakable bond" can't even begin to describe what we have, *but I will say this movie comes pretty darn close when painting the picture though.* Queue the dream sequence music ... see Sally, played by Sandra Bullock, and Gillian, played by Nicole Kidman, who are as opposite as opposite could be from one having dark hair (like me) to one having red hair (like Re). Their choices in life styles, men and identities couldn't be more opposite than the North and South Poles, and that is totally me and Re!

Let's start with Sally, a.k.a. me! She was the older sister who only wanted a perfectly normal life even if that meant ignoring who she truly was deep down inside. She was born and raised as a witch and was blessed with a gift, but didn't want to be different; she wanted to fit in with society and only wanted to be like everyone else. She denied who she was because she was so determined to be normal. She got married, had two beautiful daughters of her own, stayed in her home town and eventually opened up her own little botanical shop. As she said she was so "happy being blissfully normal." To her life was perfect.

And then there was the fiery red headed little sister, Gillian. Man, was she Re! She was intense, rebellious, eccentric, and courageous. One night, Gilly decided to leave home at a very young age because she hated it there, by escaping out her bedroom window to run off with the cute boy waiting for her down below. She wanted to go somewhere where no one had ever heard of them (*see in that town the Owens Women were known as witches for centuries*). She traveled all over the country, laying in the sun, hanging by the pool, partying all the time, living life on the edge and had a million friends ... to her life was perfect!

Although the two of them were day and night, yin and yang, black and white, they ALWAYS had each other. When Gillian was leaving home, she made a promise to Sally that they were going to grow old together. She said, "It's going to be you and me, living in this big house, these two old biddies with all these cats. I bet we even die on the same day!" And then she takes her boyfriend's pocket knife and cuts the palm of her right hand ... my blood ... then proceeds to cut the palm of Sally's left hand ... your blood ... and clasps their two hands together ... our blood! As me and Re say ... from the cradle to the grave, that was us all the way!

Animals Out The Window

Re and I grew up on a very busy street in an average little town outside of Philly, where other kids our age mostly lived on the back streets and all played with each other. Us, on the other hand, were latch-key kids and only really had each other growing up. See, our Mom had to work multiple jobs to help support the family because our Dad got laid off from the Budd plant, which really caused us to struggle. He had a tough time finding a job as a pipe fitter so he spent most of his time doing one side job after the next to get by. They both were out busting their butts for our survival, so we were pretty much on our own most of the days. Some people would see that as sad, throw pity on us or just feel bad for us; but the way I look at it, it was that experience that created the unbreakable bond that Re and I have.

Our minds worked as one, our imaginations took on shapes unexplainable to most people. As kids, we took creating games and playing to the next level ... outside of the box didn't pertain to us because there was no box in our world, *unless we made it into a clubhouse.* We didn't have much when it came to material things, but we had everything when our minds came alive. We would create paper people from cut outs found in the Sunday comics and Barbie packaging. We would entertain ourselves for hours with two plastic Easter baskets and a couple of jump ropes swinging our Snoopy and Snooper stuffed animals from one second story window to the next. Those silly games were awesome to us, our childhood together contained some of the best memories of my life. Like Sally and Gillian, whose bond grew stronger after their mother died when they were little, Re and I's indestructible relationship became iron clad tight during our alone years together too.

Apron Strings

As we got older, my sisterly role turned more into the motherly type. My Mom always said I would run around and say Re was *my* baby, and that she was. I protected her, mothered her, fought with her over crazy choices she made, and became her biggest fan. The pedestal I built to put her up on no one could touch. Through her high school years I cheered her on from the stands during competitions on a Saturday night like all the other proud parents instead of partying my butt off during my college years ... I was even on her post-prom parents' committee decorating for the big night! Without even knowing it, my life began to start being lived through her life.

Let's look at it this way, you know how Gillian in the movie wanted out of her house so bad and couldn't wait to live life, well that was my sister. She left home and began to experience life by going away to college where she met a ton of friends, pledged as a sorority sister, would party over the border in Canada on the weekends and got the taste of freedom. Me, on the other hand, I was like Sally. I lived at home with my parents, commuted to college, worked and once in a while went out with my friends if I wasn't waitressing or drawing. I was the little home-body waiting to hear all about my sister's adventures and stories just like Sally would get postcards from Gilly all the time. The older I got the more I started living through my little sister.

The 1st Time We Said "I Love You!"

As time went on, my sister went from living at college, to an apartment and then her address became The World. Mine moved only five traffic lights away. I went from living at home through college to buying a home up the street. My journey timeline went from graduating high school, to two weeks later starting college, then getting pregnant my last semester in college, graduating with a huge baby belly, to buying my Grand-mom's home, to having my daughter and getting married all before the age of 22. Talk about accomplishing things off the "normal" checklist at mock speed ... does it get anymore textbook?

While I was pouring all my time and energy into leading the "June Cleaver" lifestyle, my sister was following in our Pop-Pop's footsteps by enlisting in the Army. Man, did I become such a proud Mama! Bragging to everyone, brainwashing my kids of how amazing "The Re-Re" was, spending all my free time sending her letters and care packages during her basic training ... I became an awesome Army Wife. It was now my life's purpose!

And then one of the worst days in American history happened: 9-11. As the country was mourning such a tragedy, I was preparing for the worst thing that could ever happen to MY life ... I was sending my baby sister off to war. We had never really been separated, even through her college years, we were always chatting on the phone or she was popping home on the weekends, and now she was going to be fighting on the front lines in Iraq.

I will never forget the day my life forever changed, it was March 19th, 2002 (the 13th anniversary of my Pop-Pop's death), and it was also the day the first bombs were dropped on Iraq. We were in the basement watching it happen live when the phone rang, it was my sister. She was calling to not only ask me to send her my Pop-Pop's dog tags, but to also say good-bye, for this was going to be the last time I could hear her voice before she landed in Iraq. After that, God only knew if or when she would get the chance to do so again. In the 24 years I had my baby sister in my life, that night, that phone call, in that moment was the very first time with eyes full of tears and trembling scared voices we said "I love you" ... *she got on a plane the very next morning and then she was gone.*

With The Sweet Comes The Sour

In the movie you could see the depressing effects Gilly leaving had on Sally. Everywhere she went, leaves would fall off trees, she moped about and walked with her head down, she was sad ... she missed her sister so much! I took that to the next level. At first I was pro-active, I hung the Mother's Flag and Army Flag outside my home, covered every tree with yellow ribbons and even got my neighbors doing the same. I appeared on TV talking about her, sent the newspaper articles about her, organized and raised money to single-handedly send almost 500 Christmas stockings full of supplies over to the troops for the holidays. My life became loving and supporting my sister only!

As I built my sister's pedestal higher and higher, my emptiness began to turn into an obsession. She was my only way of life. I stopped going places because I only wanted to stay home "just in case" she called. And when I would miss her call, I would cry hysterically for hours to the point of vomiting. The only place I would show my face was at the store to buy supplies and the post office to mail them.

I became almost hermit-like. I lost over thirty pounds during the seventeen months she was gone during her first tour. The only thing I would talk about was her, not my kids, not my job, just her! I became sick, very very sick. I was in and out of doctor's offices, on a ton of meds just to get through the day, and I actually even ended up in the hospital a couple times, too. The depression consumed me. As my Mom said it was like I lost my twin, a part of me was dead inside without her.

Midnight Margaritas

After two tours in Iraq, parades, award ceremonies, bring a Vet to school days, and reporting to all the family about the different places she was stationed all over the U.S., I found my perfect niche ... I was awesome at being Re's paparazzi! I recorded almost every event that went on as her Army Wife. From photos to mementos, from decorating my Christmas tree in red, white and blue, to having my kids worship her with their Army Barbies, I was officially her biggest fan.

By this point my life was now all about her life. I loved it because I loved her. I needed her, because the only way my life was exciting was living through her. Her adventures were my adventures. My cookie cutter life sucked compared to hers in my mind. I had nothing, I did nothing, I never went anywhere, and I definitely was not shining as me. How could I when I didn't want to do anything other than polish her star!

In 2009, if you can believe it, I was having one of the roughest years of my life. I ended up losing my job that August, and things really started to spiral downward from that point forward. Little did I know that this was the beginning of my point of transition into becoming the "Real" me on my journey!

My memory is a little cloudy from all the emotional stuff going on during that time, and I am not really sure how the suggestion official-ly came about. Knowing me and Re, it was probably over Sushi and Mai Tai's (*or as we would call them after a couple drinks: Mahee Tahee's*), but Re suggested that I come out to visit her in San Francisco for the weekend that November to celebrate my birthday. She was stationed out there for schooling, I think, and she thought it would be awesome if I flew out so we could just spend me and her time together.

See as much as I don't want to admit it out loud, I always allowed the kids, my job, my husband, or whatever the reason (or excuse) would be why, to stand in the way, and I would always say, "I couldn't." Which was a load of crap! Honestly, it was actually more like I WOULDN'T do anything for myself. She was persistent about me not bailing out on this trip; even my Mom was riding my butt about going. I can hear my Mom right now saying, "Debra Ann you better get your ass on that plane before I have to drag you there by your hair!"

They were both right, I chicken out every time it comes to choosing me or doing what I want, and I almost did it again. My little one was real sick at the time, my dog wasn't doing well after being hit by a car, and I didn't have a job so I shouldn't spend the money ... as Re says ex-cuses, excuses, excuses! *I hate it when she's right ... grrrrrr!* So, I got on the plane. All by myself for the very first time in my life, I was scared out of my mind! I was so full of guilt you could pour it out of me like a gallon of milk on your cereal, but it was too late now, there was no turning back. And let me just tell you I had the time of my life!

We went to vineyards and delicious restaurants, we toured Alcatraz, we met some really amazing people everywhere we went, we saw seals and trolleys, and she took me to see the Golden Gate Bridge. We walked, not drove, walked over the Golden Gate Bridge at sunset just so I could see the sun melt into the Pacific Ocean … it was breathtaking! It will be a memory that will forever be a part of my soul. I took thousands of photos, a passion of mine that was rediscovered through this experience. Ahhhh, I felt good, I felt inspired and for the very first time in my life, I felt alive! All gifts I had never known I possessed or even deserved to have, until my sister opened the door to a whole new world that could be mine.

Clean Up Your Own Mess

I had a normal, typical, national average life, and I worked really hard to have it and that is exactly what I came home to. I just came from an experience that showed me I do have wings, and I can fly. There was a "me" buried deep down inside screaming to be freed from within that I just need to let it out. Sadly, the life I came home to reminded me real fast that this newfound self discovery was not possible in the world I created around me for all these years.

As time after the trip went on, I struggled with what I wanted my life to be and what it really was. I was unhappy. I felt stuck. I was confused and trapped between a rock and a hard place and didn't know how to change it. My trip to Cali gave me the taste of freedom, and I knew deep down inside, in my heart of hearts, the real me was festering like a little spark smoldering beneath the brush and leaves in a forest just waiting to erupt.

Month after month, I became more bitter towards my friends that seemed to be happy. I became angry and frustrated with myself and started taking my rage out on my kids and family. I had no job, no self respect, no direction and a life in limbo was really not working for me. And yes, my emotions did turn down the road of depression. I felt myself disconnecting once again. I stopped hanging out with friends because I didn't want to hear how great their freakin' lives were when mine sucked! I began clinging on to people to the point of suffocating the relationship just to feel some kind of self worth and importance. I was losing it. I had a glimpse of the real me, and I wanted it, I wanted it bad! I just didn't know how to go about getting it? Ya know how people say it takes a tragic event of some sort to make people grow and change … well, Re gave me mine!

In the movie, Gillian gets herself into this mess with a guy where her sister, Sal, has to come bail her out of it. During the fight, Sally screams' "It's all about you Gillian, I am sick and tired of cleaning up your messes." *(Stay with me here, people, this is where it gets good)* Ticked off Gillian comes back at her with, "**At least I lived my life, and you hate me for that because it scares the hell out of you!** Look at you, you spend all your energy just trying to fit in, be normal, but you're never going to fit in, Sal, because we're different, and so are your girls! All my life I wished I had half your talent. You're wasting yourself, Sal." I swear to you my sister must have written those lines for the movie, because she said those exact words to me in my living room! It was a huge, I mean a HUGE, fight, but it was a blessing in disguise and probably the best thing that ever happened to "ME."

Was she right? Was I too busy living my life through her, my kids, and my husband, that I wasn't living my own? Did I possess all this power, and I wasn't using any of it?

Was I really wasting myself?

The Light Hurts My Eyes!

Yes, yes I was wasting myself! She was right, why didn't I see all that I am like she did? It was time for me to grab hold of my own life and stop living in the shadows of my sister's. Yeah, it did scare the hell out of me, like she said, but it was my turn to step into the light and live the life "I" was meant to live. She always looked up to me and believed in me, and now it was my turn to believe in myself. She may have been the one who kicked me in the butt in order to wake me up, but it is 100% up to me to do something about it and change the life I was leading. No one can do it for me; it is all up to me!

In the past two years since Cali, I have stepped into the light and out of the shadows. I have discovered more about myself, grown as a person and have learned A LOT about who I am. I now like the person I am, I can't honestly say I totally love me because along this path to self discovery I have also learned there are things about myself that I really didn't like. I now see the things I didn't want to see before, recognizing that they are things I do not like about me and really making the effort to grow from them and change myself for the better because of them. I know there are people I have hurt along the way and through the years that I want to apologize to. I know I have done things that I regret and wish I could take back but can't. But I do know that these *are* the events and experiences that I have grown from. They needed to happen so I can live the best life possible. I want to change for myself so I may be proud of who I am at the end of the day when I lay my head down on my pillow.

I complained about so many parts of my life that I hated, and little by little I am embracing all the avenues of my life and changing them to be the way I have secretly always dreamed of. I don't fight against what I don't have any more; I now focus on all the beautiful things I DO have in my life instead. I feed those things with MY love and energy, and I watch with astonishment how the universe blesses my life with such incredible amazing things in return.

I allow myself to live my life free from constraints, judgment and fear. I am now finally happy and I no longer punish myself though guilt. I am not scared anymore to be me. I am finally empowered and am finally in control of my own life. I have my sister to thank, for not only opening the door to show me what is possible out there in the world, but for believing in me when I didn't have the courage to believe in myself.

Because of her, I now *live* my life. I now make the effort to travel and photograph all I see without making excuses of why I can't go. The other year I finally bought myself some awesome camera equipment without feeling bad because there are eight million other things I should be spending the money on. I even took the time, for myself, to take photography classes so I can better my talents and passion.

Incredible people are now entering my life who actually see me for me and are presenting me with numerous opportunities to encourage my interests. I now own my own landscape design company and am a respected figure in my field. I have even won two awards!

Oh, here is another thing ... I write. Because of my dear sweet friend, Robyn, I have discovered this newfound talent of writing, and I am actually pretty good at it. I love sharing my life's adventures with others, *ya know the things I use to complain about and hate about my life,* so they, too, may learn and grow from my experiences. It makes me happy and is very therapeutic for me.

Something I truly thought I lost about myself was my passion of being an artist. The other year, I picked up my charcoals for the first time in 20 years and drew this breath-taking picture of an eagle in the moon-lit sky. I literally stopped my "normal" world and spent hours upon hours in my creative mojo zone as if the planet stood still around me.

From there I have gone on to draw several pieces for people and looking forward to doing my very first piece for myself. I love being the artsy-fartsy type ... it's so ME!

I could go on and on about all the things I am finally doing that make me ecstatic. I finally feel in control of me, confident in my choices and happy with my life. I know that I AM finally being true to myself. Can I say I am living my best life? Hell no, but what I can say is I have just begun to live the best life I possibly can, and I know I can't wait to see what lies ahead for me on my journey! Ride the roller coaster baby and enjoy the ride!

> **From the cradle to the grave, you will**
> **always be the yin to my yang.**
> **Thank you Re, for everything!**

My story is dedicated to my sister, Heather Wright, who is and always will be my Hero. I love you, Re!

I would love to thank my amazing family whose love and support has helped make my dreams possible! My incredible daughters, Mickayla and Shawnna, whose love gives their Mommy's soul wings every day; my Ma who has always seen the best in me even when I couldn't and has never left my side on my incredible journey; and the four amazing people whose devotion, love and tenderness has helped carry me through two of the toughest years of my life (while my sister was serving her two tours in the Iraq War) Dan, Fran, Phil and my Dad … Thank You All, I wouldn't have made it through without you. And lastly, I would like to thank my baby sister, Re, and all the brave service men and women who proudly serve and protect this great country of ours every day!

~ Deb Wright

Elizabeth Candlish

ELIZABETH CANDLISH is an author and the owner of Intuitive Heart, who is a licensed Heal Your Life® Workshop Leader and Life Coach. Elizabeth is also the owner of Sunshine Reiki Healing Centre, a Usui/Karuna Reiki Master/Teacher/Practitioner, Chartered Herbalist, Bach Flower Remedy Practitioner, and has been helping clients over many years heal from within.

Elizabeth lives on the beautiful Sunshine Coast, Vancouver with her wonderful husband Martin. Elizabeth is passionate about her work and in her spare time enjoys writing, gardening, spending time with friends and family and loves traveling around the world with Martin.

eacandlish@dccnet.com
www.elizabethcandlish.com

Home From Home

We have not always lived in Canada; in fact, we came to live in Canada because of a two-week holiday over 17 years ago in October, 1995. My husband, Martin, and I went on a holiday to Vancouver, BC Canada for two weeks. Little did we know then that our holiday in Canada would completely change our lives for the better and so much more.

We had a wonderful holiday adventure driving around and relaxing just enjoying this wonderful country. Even though it rained for 12 days out of the two weeks, we both loved the mountains, beaches, the tourist sights. I fell in love with the greenery, trees, trails, and the quiet. It felt so peaceful no matter where we went, and everywhere was so much bigger than in England. Everything was so very different to where we were living at that time, and we both fell in love with Canada; it felt like home from home.

In fact, a few days after we arrived home, I went down to the local stores. I parked my car on one of the side streets, walked down to the stores and had this huge feeling that I did not belong there anymore. It was such a strange feeling, but for some reason I did not feel this was where I was meant to be living. I could not walk in any of the stores. It was a scary feeling – I had no idea what was happening. A huge shift had happened to me.

I turned around and went home and told Martin about my experience. Even though we had often talked about emigrating and moving to another country to start a new life, up to this point we had just been talking about it, but nothing serious. After much discussion, we felt that this was the perfect opportunity for us, and if we were going to do something about it, then this was the moment to start planning. It had to be now, the timing felt as if it was the right time to do this. I like to think we chose Canada, but in reality, I think Canada chose us.

We started the process of applying to immigrate to Canada. Some computer research revealed that it was based on a points system. When we worked out the points, we discovered that we had more than enough points needed to apply, which was good news to start off with. We then sent for the immigration kit which was the next step. It took a couple of weeks for that to come through in the mail.

As soon as it arrived, we began the long process of filling in applications forms and putting together all the documentation that was needed for this long process: marriage certificates, birth certificates, college certificates. Martin completed all the paper work; he is good at things like that. Gathering all the required documents together took a few weeks, then we sent our immigration forms off with our registration fee to the Canadian Immigration Office in London to apply to live in Canada, again keeping our fingers crossed that our dream would be granted. We had no idea how long it would take, but that was okay, the time would be right for us when it did happen. I could see and feel us living in Canada no matter how long it was going to take.

It was a long process with papers going back and forth for months. About three months passed with no communication at all. That was the hard part the waiting, the not knowing what was happening. Was our application being accepted or rejected? Then one morning we received papers for a medical checkup for each of us; by the time these papers arrived we started to get a good feeling about this.

Getting through to the Medical stage was a huge accomplishment in itself, we had to have blood tests, x rays and more tests. This was to make sure we were in optimum health. This also meant we had reached the next stage of the immigration process, we knew we were one step closer to living in Canada. We both passed the medical, and then the wait began for our interview – again, we heard nothing for quite a few weeks.

Then one morning we woke up to find a letter had come through our mailbox with the date for our interview, which was a couple of weeks away and which was to be held in London. The excitement was building up now. As you can imagine, on the five-hour drive down to London, we were both very nervous.

We attended the immigration interview where we were asked many questions and were able to answer them all. In addition, they asked for us to provide more documentation, certificates which they needed before we could proceed any further. We were not aware that they needed any more information so this was frustrating as we thought we had given them everything they needed and had asked for. We left on that day still uncertain as to whether we would be accepted or rejected, and at the same time knew we were one step closer once we were able to put the documentation together and put in the mail to them.

Martin was able to provide the documentation that was required, but it took a few weeks to locate all the information that was needed. One of the colleges Martin had attended from many years ago had closed down, complicating the process. He did lots of research and with patience and perseverance, all the needed documentation was found so that we could proceed with our application.

Again, time went by with no communication although by this time we were fortunate that Martin was working down in London, so he was able to go to the Immigration Office in person during his lunchtime, to check on the status of all the required documentation. We felt that maybe there was something else that they needed, because you never know when a letter might get lost in the mail.

Martin was able to talk to someone in the Canada House and was told that they were indeed waiting for another document, but we had received no letters or telephone calls about it. We were very lucky he had checked, then when he came home he found the document that they requested, and he was able to drop it in to them by hand the following week. Now things could move forward.

Again, weeks went by with no response so Martin went back to their office a second time to ask if they needed anything else. This time he was told no, they had everything they needed, and the application was in the process of being accepted for us to live in Canada. He was also told that we would receive the paperwork in the mail.

This was wonderful news! The day he walked into that office was actually a few days before Christmas, and would you believe it – on Christmas Eve we received the official papers that we had been granted approval to immigrate to Canada.

We now had six months in which to put our plans together for the move. What a wonderful and exciting Christmas gift for both of us, and what a relief from the stress of the past eighteen months of filling in forms, and waiting for news. We were now just a flight away from living in Canada, but still a lot of preparing and planning to do.

Although we had told family and friends about going to live in Canada, now we had the official, exciting news about our new life. Before, I don't think anyone really believed we would make the move. Our children, Steve and Cheryl, had already decided they did not want to move from the UK to live in Canada. At that time they wanted to stay with their friends, and, in fact, had no idea what Canada was like. After all, if their parents were going to live there, it must be really old fashioned and not much fun. How wrong could they be! We had known from the beginning of the process of applying to live in Canada that they didn't want to come with us. I was always hoping they would change their minds, but they didn't and that was their choice. This was really hard to hear, but at the same time I knew they were responsible adults, and if they were happy with their decision, then I tried to be happy with them.

Martin and I then sat down and started planning for our new life in Canada. We also had a lovely Lhasa Apso dog named Boomer, and we were taking him with us to Canada. We only had him for about 18 months, and he was a great little dog with such a wonderful personality and such great company. At least he couldn't say he didn't want to go with us, and it was so good to be able to take him with us. Boomer couldn't replace Steve or Cheryl, but he was family to us, and I knew he would be great company for us.

We then made contact with our vet so Boomer could have his own checkups and injections, and filled in the appropriate forms so he could immigrate together with us. We also had to get a crate built for him for the flight, and made arrangements for that to be done. Boomer was so lucky and so were we, as Canada does not have quarantine rules so he could fly on the same flight as us, and he would come to our new home to live with us without any separation, except for the flight.

We then started phoning shipping and removal companies for prices for shipping furniture, and clothes to Canada. We then started to go through our home to decide what to take with us and what to leave behind. As Steve and Cheryl were staying behind, we knew they would use the majority of what we were leaving and that they would share it out between themselves. We just wanted to take what was sentimental to us, and what we would need to start up a new home.

Even though it was an exciting time and a new chapter in our lives, the doubts did creep in though every now and again. Questions came up, such as:

- What if we didn't like it over in Canada? But I would remind myself how we loved it over there, and it was a wonderful opportunity for us.

- Was it just a holiday place and not right for us? Again I would tell myself how we loved it there, and I would remember how I felt while we were in Canada.

- Would I get homesick? On and on the doubts were there.

- Where was home going to be? We had no idea where we would live yet.

But despite the questions, at the end of the day, we decided that it was the right thing to do. And, hey, if either of us didn't like it, we could always go back to the UK so we had nothing to lose at all.

What I did realize though, was that I did not want was to be sitting in a chair in the UK 10 years from now, not having taken this wonderful opportunity to go and live in Canada and then have to say to myself, "What if we had gone to Canada? I wonder what our life would have been like now." I knew that if things did not work out, and I was homesick I could go back, but it turned out that never happened to either of us.

We set a date a few days after Mother's Day, March 10, 1997, to fly to Canada. This was really only a few weeks away! A week after Christmas in January, we had more good news. One of the newspapers had a special offer that if you collected coupons, you could buy one ticket to fly anywhere in the world and get the other ticket free with the coupons. Of course, we collected the coupons so it was a huge saving for us.

What a gift, as if the Universe was saying: "You have made the right decision, and here is a free ticket to help you on your way."

On March 10, 1997, when the big day came, I was so emotional. Friends and family were phoning us to wish us luck, but I could not speak on the phone because no one could understand me I was sobbing so much. I hate goodbyes. I even cry when I drop people off at the airport, or even picking them up. I was finding it hard to let go, but I knew that it was the right thing for us to do. What made it a bit easier for us was that Cheryl and Steve were coming with their partners to Canada for a two-week holiday in June. They came over and had a great time. Steve loved it so much, he came to live in Canada four years after we did and now lives in Alberta.

We flew out of the London airport and arrived in Vancouver in the evening of March 10, 1997. (UK is eight hours ahead of Canada.) We went through the immigration process fairly quickly . We then collected Boomer who was waiting for us in his crate. He was so excited to see us after spending time in the crate and not knowing where he was or where he was going.

When we arrived, it was snowing, we had nowhere to live, no jobs, and Boomer with us. What we did not realize, and no one had mentioned to us in our planning, is that it is very difficult to find somewhere to live if you have a pet or children. (Things have changed a lot since then.)

Martin went to the Tourist Information to find out about accommodations at maybe a hotel or B&B where we could stay for a few nights until we had gotten over our travel tiredness and jet lag. The man at the tourist desk got chatting to Martin and called over a friend of his who was there at the airport dropping off friends. What a lovely lady she turned out to be. He explained to her that we had just arrived in Vancouver. For his friend to be there at exactly the same time was another one of the amazing, synchronistic things that happened to us.

Martin came back over to me as I was waiting with Boomer and told me we had somewhere to stay for a few nights and Boomer could stay with us as well. Great news! This lovely lady even drove us, through the snow, to her rental apartment, which was on the 7th floor and overlooked Vancouver city centre. What a beautiful sight to see all the lights over Vancouver brightly lit up surround with snow.

We relaxed for a few days and contacted our family to let them know we had arrived safely and that everything was good. The next task was to find somewhere more permanent to live which we did, we found a lovely home in West Vancouver.

Martin found a great job within a few weeks, and I found a job as well. I have often been told that no matter what work you did in the UK, your career would change in Canada. I found that to be very true for myself. I was a PA/Secretary in the UK, and I became a receptionist for a physiotherapy clinic, then I trained to become a Medical Office Assistant. I loved working in a doctor's office, and I did that for a few years. I now work for myself and own my own business on the beautiful Sunshine Coast, Vancouver.

We became Canadian citizens four years after arriving in Canada. Both of us love living in Canada; in fact, Martin has only been back to the UK once since we moved to Canada. I, on the other hand, go over every year as Cheryl, my daughter, still lives there with Josh and Fin, my two wonderful grandsons, and I go to see them as much as I can. My dream is for all my family to live in Canada one day.

Although our lives changed, it was for the better, and we are now living the life we dreamed about. Sometimes, we have to step out of our comfort zone to step into our best life!

To my brother Dave McFadden - I miss you so much and think of you every day. You were taken away from us far too soon. It would have been great had your dreams come true, and you came to live in Canada, too, but it was not meant to be.

To Martin for being the perfect travel partner, without you I would not have taken the opportunity to come to live in Canada. You have made our dreams come true.

Many thanks to Nancy Newman and Lisa Hardwick for making my dreams come true by allowing me this wonderful opportunity in sharing my stories with the world. I love you both very much.

~ Elizabeth Candlish

Dena DeLuco

Photo Credit: Jaci Clark Photography

DENA DELUCO is a passionate and inspiring teacher, who has an exceptional gift for helping people get "unstuck." Her compelling workshops merge together Ancient Wisdom, Modern Science and Universal Laws and Principles, translating into paradigm-blasting tools which help uncover hidden gifts and talents; adding new dimension and purpose.

dena@minddeva.com
www.minddeva.com

The Three Epiphanies

When was the last time you encountered something that completely changed your life or shifted your perspective? Perhaps it was a brilliant nugget of profound wisdom that leapt off the page of a book, an awe-inspiring speaker who plunged into the depths of your being, a late night conversation with a dear friend, or even your own inner dialog.

Whatever the method of delivery, that bit of life-changing knowledge was your epiphany, and it uncovered a magic door that led you into a deeper awareness. Like an enchanted movie scene, your moment unfolded in slow motion, revealing a rich new truth. You almost expected the heavens to open and the sun to drench the earth in magnificent golden rays, while a chorus of angels joined in a glorious chorus. Even if it didn't quite play out that way, it felt just as good.

I have been fortunate to experience many epiphanies. In fact, the older I get, the more often they seem to come! This is my inspiration for writing.

In the time it takes to curl up on a cozy couch and enjoy a nice cup of coffee, I'd like to share three lessons, or epiphanies, that I have learned … okay … *continue* to learn. I spent the first forty-some years of my life doing it "the hard way." Call it what you will: roadblocks, school of hard knocks, detours or (my personal favorite), *the scenic route*. Since I have learned these three simple lessons, my life flows with much more ease and grace. It is my sincere hope that my "Epiphanies" will inspire you to walk your path with even more poise and elegance, and that they will support and serve *you* on *your amazing journey.*

Epiphany 1: Fear Vs. Excitement

When I was just six years old, a Monster lived beneath my bed. He was red, had long, dirty fingernails and one ... big ... bloodshot eye. The more I tried to push him out of my thoughts ... the bigger he got. The harder I prayed he would leave me alone, the more real he became. But I tried and I prayed, and I prayed and I tried ... until finally, I was certain ... that I could now hear him breathing. I could smell the foul stench of his breath ... with each tick of the clock that darned Monster got bigger and uglier.

When I could no longer tolerate his torment, I would scream, "Daddy! *DAD-DY!*" My gentle giant would softly come to my bedside. Armed with his trusty flashlight, we would pierce through the darkness beneath the pale pink, lace dust ruffle that skirted my bed. Much to my surprise (and delight), we found no Monster. No, the only thing lurking beneath my bed was one renegade Barbie Doll (with a really bad haircut), a green crayon and a dust bunny.

Does this ring a bell? Did you have a Monster beneath your bed (or maybe hiding in the closet)? Personally, I lived with a debilitating fear of that wretched Monster. In fact, this Monster called Fear would become my personal pattern for many decades ... yes, even into adulthood. He took many shapes over the years, but the Monster himself showed up through all phases of my life. Perhaps He has followed you through life as well.

How do we come to grips with fear? How does it mold our lives? How can we make friends with the Monster under the bed? Read on ... this is where it gets good!

A few years ago, a coaching/hypnosis client (I'll call her Suzie) came to me for a session. When asked, "What would you like to work on today?" Suzie sat up tall in the chair, confidently pushed her chest out and announced, "I want you to eliminate all fear from my life." On the outside, I remained calm, poised. On the inside, I was giving her spiritual high-fives, blessings and salutations. It was brilliant! Why had I never thought of it? What couldn't I accomplish if I had no fear?

After a moment of quiet reflection (and awe-inspiring, unspoken kudos), I allowed my mind to consider her request. I found myself telling Suzie, "FEAR is not always a bad thing. In fact, Fear keeps us from harm's way; the proverbial edge of the cliff ... or hand from the hot stove." After a short deliberation, we concluded that bringing forward Suzie's innate resources to *overcome the fear* offered a better solution. Instead of *exterminating* all fear, we unleashed her natural abilities and brought them into her conscious awareness. Suzie left my office that day, empowered, inspired and liberated. We had uncovered some of her natural resources to help shine a light on fear. As for me, I left with more questions!

Yes, fear can be a "good thing." There had to be more to it though. What about that pesky "Monster under the bed" fear? This Monster is NOT the same fear which keeps us from harm's way. No, *this* fear holds us tightly within the confines of our comfort zone. This fear disconnects us from our true Divine nature ... the essence of who we truly are!

Perplexed by this new information, I spent the days and weeks following Suzie's session in deep contemplation. Finally, during an early morning meditation, I asked the question, "What is the purpose of this "Monster under the bed" fear in my life?" To my surprise, the answer came almost instantly. I remembered a yoga class from at least a year before. The instructor claimed that, "Fear and excitement feel the same in the body." She continued, *"Fear is simply excitement without breath."*

The meaning was completely lost to me at the time, but now, maybe I could finally make sense of it. I knew I was on to something BIG. Yes, fear and excitement DO *feel* the same. But I took it one step further. What if they *are* the same? How could this be? Could it be that THIS fear is actually an indication, a marker if you will, that something bigger, stronger, more powerful is seeking to emerge through you? Could it be that this Monster known as fear is actually a signal from your Higher Self, or even your very Soul, that you have just encountered a situation or challenge you are now fully equipped to conquer? Maybe all these years, I was just mistaking the identity of the Monster.

And so I began a thorough process of re-labeling, re-categorizing each memory that involved the Monster named Fear. I worked ardently. I organized each old memory of fear into two groups. (I didn't actually write each fear down; I just acknowledged the memory as I recalled it.) On one side was the "edge of the cliff" fear. This self-defense mechanism had served me well over the years. On the other side stood the "Monster under the bed" fear. This was the fear that plagued me through all of my childhood and well into my adult life. This was the thorn in my side, the curse that had to be eliminated! And now, just like Suzie, I was prepared to fight that Monster! Little did I know at the time, this Monster was to become my favorite friend *and* enemy ... my *frienemy!*

After reassigning many old fears to a place of better understanding, I trained myself to re-label them *on the fly*. Any time I became aware of fear, I asked myself, "Is this an 'edge of the cliff' fear or a 'Monster under the bed' fear?" When I recognized the Monster fear, I practiced shifting my perception from *fear* to *excitement*. Something magical began to happen. I started to *thank* the fear for alerting me to the situation. After a short time, I could actually notice a difference in my ability to discern these two types of fear. It truly WAS excitement! And with the excitement came a new confidence. Sweet Liberation! This practice has now become a wonderful habit and serves me in countless ways.

Fear and excitement ... feel the same in the body! I invite you to notice the distinction in *your* awareness! When you detect a Monster hiding beneath *your* bed, expose him to the light of truth. It may be that he brings the gift of growth and sweet success to a challenging situation, a reminder that you have within you every resource needed to expand your comfort zone! As I close Epiphany One, I leave you with a famous quote from one of our great leaders:

> ❧ So, first of all, let me assert my firm belief that the only thing we have to fear ... is fear itself – nameless, unreasoning, unjustified terror which paralyzes needed efforts to convert retreat into advance.
>
> ~ FRANKLIN D. ROOSEVELT
> (DURING HIS INAUGURAL SPEECH, 1933)

Epiphany Two: If It Doesn't Honor You, It's Not Your Truth!

Epiphany Two came to me, courtesy of Sandra Taylor. I had read her book, *Quantum Success*, several years ago. It helped me understand the "science" behind the ever-popular *Law of Attraction* that everyone had been talking about. (Yes, I am one of those semi-nerdy girls who just *has* to understand "how things work.")

I was driving to my office, listening to a CD of a workshop Sandy had presented in Cleveland, Ohio. And, as if talking directly to me, I heard these words, "If it doesn't honor you, it's not your truth." It was like slow motion, instant replay, " ... If ... it ... doesn't ... honor ... you ... it's ... not ... your ... truth ... !" This simple phrase, in some mystical way, had given me "permission" to let go of any belief that wasn't honoring to myself, or to my life.

Sandy further explained that you have the *right* and the *responsibility* to change any belief that does not honor you. Just then I think I actually heard the heavenly choir of angels! I can change my beliefs? Any belief? *Epiphany!* I thought that beliefs were embedded, encoded, programmed into us. I always thought that our beliefs *are* our truths. And ... that we are stuck with them! You mean I could CHOOSE my beliefs? I realized then that the beliefs I had held all my life that did not honor me were just fabrications, deceptions, misrepresentations ... mis-information.

And, just like the "Monster under the bed" process, I began to filter my entire belief system. Any (yes, ANY) belief that did not survive the "does this honor me" clause, was simply upgraded, deleted or re-placed with a new, empowering truth! There were so many beliefs I held about myself. In fact, most of what I believed about "me" did not honor me. Two years later, I am just now getting to a place that this process has become more of a habit than a full time job!

What old, limiting beliefs do you hold about yourself? Maybe some were just in your "DNA" ... you know, handed down from your family or heritage. Others may have been born from a place of fear or mis-in-formation. No matter how they originated, once you become conscious of them, you have the power to create a new belief about yourself (or those around you) that is more honoring and loving.

Let me share a gentle caution that accompanies Epiphany Two. It is important to reframe our old beliefs (misinformation) from a place of *no guilt* and *no blame*. It is easy to point the finger at those "teachers" who "gifted" us with our old beliefs. This serves no one. It doesn't matter *how* the dishonoring belief came to be. That means no judgment on you for *accepting* the belief, and no blame to the one(s) who *gave* the belief to you. Guilt and blame just create more mis-information. The old, limiting beliefs aren't necessarily good or bad; maybe it's just time for them to be consciously upgraded.

In a nutshell, a belief is merely a thought that you hold in your mind. The law of life is the law of belief. Your thoughts (and the emotions and actions which accompany them) are creative. By changing, or rather by *choosing*, a better or more empowering belief, it stands to reason that you will experience better, more empowering results. If you are unsure of your beliefs … simply take a look at your results. That's a great place to start! (Remember, no judgment … that's the tricky part!)

Epiphany Three: Your Past ≠ Your Future

I spent over half of my life in the role of the victim. I carried my "stories" (and fears) around with me everywhere I went. "My parents divorced; my mom moved away … I had to grow up too fast … My ex-husband abused and mistreated me … I don't know what I am supposed to do with my life … If God would just tell me my purpose, I would do it." These were just a few of *my* stories (my identities). These were *my* "reasons" (*excuses*) for not having the life I wanted. And, in our society, each one is considered an acceptable reason for being angry, fearful … lost, acceptable reasons for staying small.

Who is to blame for *your* limitations? What stories do you hold on to? And if letting them go would help you move forward … would you let them go? What if your past held no power over your future? Imagine what your life could look like! Today holds the opportunity to begin again; start over with a clean slate (like a virtual "do-over"). No, not at the beginning; with nothing ... Today as you "start again," you bring with you all of the lessons learned, all of the joy, the knowledge, the wisdom, the mutually loving relationships – everything in your life that makes it wonderful, inspiring, fun and adventurous.

So, you may be wondering ... what is left behind? Great question! As you begin again, you have permission to leave behind all of the "mis-information" about who you truly are. You can leave behind the fear, doubt and worry. Leave behind the "I'm not smart enough, pretty enough, skinny enough, rich enough" ... any *not enough-ness* that comes into your awareness. That is, essentially *any*thing in your old, limiting programming that no longer serves you... That's what you leave behind. And, as you leave behind the lack and limitation of your past, you begin anew, refreshed, energized ... inspired!

You are a unique and wonderful expression of pure potential! Nothing holds you back except the reasons, stories (dare I say, *excuses*) of why you can't, the limiting beliefs which were "gifted" to you before you were old enough to filter them ... Imagine your life without limitations, without the baggage of your youth, without the fear, doubt, worry and limitations.

Your past is only a story ... unless you choose it to be your identity. And, even if it's been your identity for years (or like me ... *decades*) you have the resources (right now) to let it go! When will you choose to let it go? We all fall down. We all get stuck. It's what we do after we fall that determines who we become. If you are like most, you eventually DO get up, but then comes the self-loathing, shame and relentless internal dialog of condescension. I still catch myself playing this game ... no judgment, it's just *habit*. The sooner we notice the game, and let it go ... the more gracefully we can move through life.

So many clients say to me, "If I could just be *where you are*, I could be happy." Or, "If I could just get past this detour or maneuver that roadblock ... that's where I'll find my bliss." And my personal favorite ... "I'll be okay when I hit the lottery." Money, relationships, careers ... these are all just "magnifiers." Let me explain. If you are already truly happy, and more money comes your way ... you will probably become happier. However, if you are miserable ... and more money comes along, you have the potential for more misery! The same goes for relationships, success in business, etc.

True and lasting happiness is a *practice*. It's not contingent on "things" or circumstance. Most of us have figured this out on a conscious level, but it's a challenge to integrate it into our marvelous "deep mind." You know ... the one that guides us through life. Again, this is about practice ... persistent, consistent, *conscious* practice. We spend so much of our time caught up in our own stories of blame, that often the truth of *who* we are (our true identity) goes unnoticed.

Of course, for most of us, we can spot the majestic fundamental nature of *others* a mile away. When asked about our own Divine essence ... usually it's not even a blip on our radar! It is so very easy, entirely simple for me to catch a glimmer of *your* higher available resources ... not so easy to see my own. That is, until very recently.

> ❧ I am learning that each magical NOW that comes my way holds an opportunity for incredible outcomes.
>
> ~ DENA DELUCO

I am learning (making it a conscious practice) to trust myself. *I am learning that each magical NOW that comes my way holds an opportunity for incredible outcomes.* And ... the more I choose what looks (or feels) like the *most empowering and loving perspective* (currently available in my sea of not-so-limited thinking), the more gracefully I maneuver through life. So now, instead of "spending" time ... I am gratefully "investing" time. It might seem to be a minute distinction, but there are massive fundamental transforming qualities within the latter.

 The measure of a man's strength is not what God is willing to give him, but what he himself has the will and the intelligence to appropriate to himself. God gives you all there is. The only question you have is ... how much are you willing to take of the unlimited supply?

~ WALLACE D. WATTLES

I invite you to bask in the feeling of being supported by, connected to, an Infinite Supply. Remember, *you are unlimited potential*, just waiting to be realized!

TAKE ACTION!

 You stand at the doorway of creation; the threshold of choice.

~ DENA DELUCO

YOU have a high and noble calling. What legacy will you leave? Who will you inspire? You have *this* magnificent life to live. *Why not live full on, wholeheartedly, holding nothing back?* It's not too late; you're just getting started! Falling down is a part of life. Getting stuck is, too. It's the getting up ... and moving forward ... that's where we take control of our destiny!

You stand at the doorway of creation; the threshold of choice. In fact, each day holds this enchanted opportunity. Truth be told, each *moment* holds this possibility. The *"now"* is all we really have. The past is gone. The future is merely an illusion, a magical fantasy, until it becomes the *"now."* NOW is where life is lived! *Now* is where the magic happens. If the only thing holding you back is your story of why "you can't" ... are you willing to let it go?

My invitation to you is to allow yourself to become aware of the fears, the old limiting beliefs, stories, reasons and excuses that hold you back. Become aware of that pesky Monster lurking beneath your bed and expose him to the light of truth. Reframe the feeling of fear and transform it into *excitement*. It could be that what you thought was "fear" is actually an indication that you have just met a life challenge that you are now ready to tackle, fully equipped with every resource needed for success!

Begin a process of examining the foundations of your belief system. Keep in mind that any principle that you hold in your beliefs which does not honor or empower you, does not have to be true for you anymore. You have the right and the responsibility for an upgrade!

And lastly – today, *this day ... this moment*, holds the opportunity for small or profound change. Your future is not doomed to be a repeat of your past ... that is, unless you choose it. By *not choosing* ... well, you may just be destined to let history repeat itself. *Reclaim your life's direction!* Allow new light to shine into your life. Whatever you carried into this moment does not need to go with you into the next! You are a unique expression of unlimited potential! Give up your story of *why you can't*, embrace the truth that, *yes, yes you can!* Give yourself permission to step into *your* best life!

Dedicated to my courageous clients, who teach me more than words can convey; to my amazing friends who keep me filled with laughter and hope; and to my loving family, whose kindness and support inspires me to greater heights.

To my teachers whose wisdom and willingness to share their stories have opened magical doors to my personal unfoldment. To Robyn Podboy for her encouragement and inspiration to write my chapter. Thanks to Joy DeSalvo, Kathy Hammons and the ladies of VIP (Nancy and Lisa) for their kindness and support. To 'Crystal Deana' (Tareshawty) whose remarkable vision and generosity help foster personal and spiritual development. To all of my 'Mountain Movers' who continually prove that with love and intention we are unlimited in potential! To the GW, each an awakening goddess. To my 'extended' family (The DeLuco clan), I treasure each and every one of you. To my extraordinary parents (Bill, Joan, Ann & Tom) and my amazing son, Isaac, I adore you more than words. And to my loving husband, Vince ... your love and support mean the world to me. BTW Tee ... yes, you truly 'do it all'!

~ Dena DeLuco

Take the first step
in faith. You don't
have to see the
whole staircase, just
take the first step.

~ MARTIN LUTHER KING, JR.

David Nixon

Photo Credit: D.M. Smith

David Nixon is a husband and father of four great children; he is an active member of one the largest nonprofit originations in the world. He enjoys helping others find their passion in life and encouraging them to LIVE THEIR DREAMS?

He resides in Hubbard, Oregon where he enjoys spending time with his family and friends. He has a real passion for dramatic storms and sitting on the beach listening to all the powerful sounds of Sea. He sincerely believes that the key to one's happiness lies within them and that they truly have a purpose in this life.

dnixon@mail.com

The Moon Will Rise

Life isn't easy is it? I know for me this has been true. I have thought about that saying a lot, and why it is that it rings so true with me. I will tell you that one of the main reasons I have struggled with my place in this world is: Comparisons.

Since as far back as I can remember, I have been comparing my life with that of others around me, not just people I knew personally, but also those I had never met – like people I would see on television. Thankfully because of my ability or my drive to find out why that is, I have picked up certain characteristics. I have been able to take a look at the root of this behavior and where it started to develop.

I know from my experience thus far, that recognizing where this behavior started is, in fact, the key to finding personal freedom to just be who I am without expectation. Life is a mysterious thing, and really, for most of us, it can be built on a foundation of uncertainty. There are many things that occur as children, which can leave us with more questions than answers that is for sure.

For me, my desire to be something other than what I was started when I was just a little tyke, sometime after my mom gave my alcoholic father the 'BOOT' and decided she would much rather raise me and my three older sisters on her own, than have to continue to deal with all the chaos and uncertainty that comes from being married to a problematic drinker.

Shortly after that, I began to realize that we were different than most families in the early 70's, who stayed married rather than deal with the stigma of being divorced. I recognized early on that people did treat us differently when they realized my mother was a single parent, and I am sure this is when my need to be something I wasn't began.

Eventually my mother remarried, and although I longed desperately for a Dad, it wasn't long before I realized he was not the one I was hoping for.

It surely isn't an easy time, adolescence that is, and at 10 years of age I had already become very unhappy with who I was and the life I had been given.

Right around this time though, I met Alice ...

We shared the 4th and 5th grade. She had long straight blonde hair, blue eyes and a smile that was contagious.

I remember we would sit with each other at lunch every day, and she was my playmate at recess. If we weren't hangin' around on the monkey bars, then we were sitting on the pea gravel making designs in the little rocks with our fingers. We actually rarely talked at all – we didn't have to. We just liked being together.

I loved her, whatever that meant at that age, but I know she felt the same way. I am certain that one of the reasons I was so drawn to this special little playmate was because she accepted me for who I was, and nothing about my life mattered to her. We just liked each other period.

Alice was like wearing my favorite pair of shoes or Saturday cartoons, nothing mattered when I was with her and life was good whenever she was around.

I remember once we had a film in class, although I can't remember what it was about. Alice and I sat next to one another and held hands, or at least fingers, through the entire thing. It felt as if my heart would beat through my chest.

Alice also gave me my first Valentine with the letters: SWAK on the envelope. I didn't know what this meant and had to ask one of my older sisters. She explained that it meant "sealed with a kiss." Wow! I couldn't believe it, but I remember knowing for sure that she felt for me as I did for her.

She was also the first girl I would call on the telephone from home. Once again we would hardly talk, but would manage to stay on the line for what seemed like forever if our parents would let us. My mom would say: "David, are you guys gonna talk or just breathe at each other?"

The Summer after 5th grade, my folks announced that we would be moving to Oregon. This was a huge shock! After all, I had been in Arizona my whole life.

I didn't know how I would tell Alice. I remember being scared and unsure how to even say it. I didn't even know where Oregon was, but I knew there were a few states in between.

So, on a Saturday I called Alice to see if we could meet at the park. We would often met there at other times, and we would ride our bikes there then toss a Frisbee or just sit in the grass and pull at the summer strands. She agreed to meet me. I remember on the ride there trying to memorize what I would say then forgetting everything as soon as I saw her.

We played chase and tetherball for a couple of hours, before she mentioned that she should head back home. I had a huge lump in my throat, the kind that no matter how hard I would swallow, I couldn't get down. She got on her bike and started to ride away and somehow I found my voice and called to her. "Alice!!! I am moving away!" She stopped with her back to me and one foot on the ground, but didn't turn around. I ran to her. I stood facing her with my hands atop hers as she gripped the handle bars shaking a little.

She just stood there staring at me, just staring at me with her eyes darting all around my face. I said again, my voice shaking, "I am moving to Oregon at the end of summer." She didn't say a word. Her face became bright red, and her eyes welled up with tears. Her bike fell to the ground, and she wrapped her arms around me so tight it was hard for me to breath. Alice tried her best to explain to me that my parents called her parents who had told her last night. She didn't want to talk about it, because then it would become real.

She said she loved me for the first time, and I knew it was true, cuz I could feel it all over me. We stood there for quite some time just holding each other. After a while Alice pulled away and dried her face on my T-shirt.

I did my best to explain to her the whole deal, how my new dad got a job offer up there, and I would have to move before the beginning of school.

Alice and I made a pact that day. We would write a letter every day and send it to each other once a week.

After I moved, we exchanged letters just as we promised for quite a few months; however, after a while the letters became more infrequent, and to this day I can't recall who sent the last one, but eventually they just stopped.

I still think of Alice from time to time and hope she is doing well. I hope that she has a husband who loves her and children, too. You know, the works. All of it, the whole deal.

Even after 30 some years, I still remember Alice as the best part of that time in my life. The thing is I don't have any desire to see her again. She had her time and place in my life, and it was wonderful. Although to you this portion of this little tale may seem somewhat sad, I am so grateful to have known her. She came into my life at just the right time. I needed her then, and I'd like to think she needed me, too. She is one of those special few who left their finger prints on my soul ...

Of course, time continued, life continued, and somehow I managed to make it into adulthood. I have since recognized that all my experiences, good and bad, up to this point in time have brought me to this place in my life where I have been able to find peace and a real absolution for just being who I am in this moment, and I am comfortable with me.

Another one of those experiences that helped bring me to this place in my life today was when I was in my early 20's, 23 at most. It was winter, late December; a day or so before the New Year. The exact date eludes me, because at this particular time in my life, I had never felt more lost and confused than any other time up this point in my life. I could easily lose days, weeks and even months at a time, just trying to avoid taking a look at where I was in that moment in time. It was a time in my life that not only was I riddled with guilt for mistakes I had made, but also I felt as if I had been dealt a bad hand.

I don't remember the exact date, but I do remember this moment like it was yesterday: we had snow that Christmas, and I remember it was still fresh on the ground. It was late in the evening, and I was back at my folk's house. My sister, Kathryn, her husband and first born had recently moved up here to Oregon from Arizona and were living with my folks hoping for a fresh start.

Although my sister wasn't aware of it, we shared this need for a fresh start in common. I had always looked up to her and actually still do, even 20 years later. I don't think her being there at that time in my life was a coincidence either, and I would like to think I was there for her as well.

That particular night I was feeling more restless than usual, and I was having a hard time quieting my thoughts. Everyone was asleep, and the house was very quiet. It was just me, and at that time of my life, I was not the best company, if you get my meaning. I decided to take a walk and clear my head.

I often did this when I was out at my folks' place. They had a fairly good chunk of property, 20 acres in the country to be exact. They purchased it shortly after we had transplanted from Arizona when I was 11, and it was truly like a little slice of Heaven with a creek and an abundance of timber, like Fir, Cedar and Alder.

After I got over the shock of our initial move from the only place I ever knew of as my home, I eventually grew to love this place. I would spend all day exploring the woods as a youth, and no matter how often I did, there seemed to always be something new for me to see. When I look back on that time in my life, it is always a good feeling. I had chickens to care for, a beautiful horse and not a care in the world. For a time I was free, free to be me. Hahaha!

I can still remember stepping out of the house, I remember how the fresh, cool air felt on my face, and the feeling as my lungs filled with that first inhale of untainted crisp air. I stepped off our front porch, and the snow crunched beneath my feet. It seemed louder than it should, as the only other sound was that of the creek that ran through this little piece of paradise. I stood there for a moment, as I often did at night and closed my eyes, to feel the rush of the quiet penetrate deep within me.

I remember just standing there with my eyes closed, and my head tilted towards the sky, just absorbing the essence of where I was. I remember the feeling of complete joy and gratitude as I opened my eyes to the night sky. Through the tall trees it seemed as if every star that could possibly be seen had been brought out just for me to gaze upon! I am sure you have witnessed those clear nights without the intrusion of unnatural light pollution; this is how it was out here, on this night.

I didn't have a flash light, but the white of the snow seemed to have a soft glow as it reflected the starlight, that allowed my eyes to easily adjust and I could see quite well. I didn't notice the moon, although I wasn't looking for it, still I was aware that I didn't see it. I began to walk down the long driveway that led from my parents' home as it rounded upward, leading to the gravel road that connected with the main road that everyone, who had been fortunate enough to stumble upon this incredibly serene piece of the world, would use to get to the rest of civilization.

I had my hands buried deep within the pockets of a pair of my favorite jeans, to shield them from the cold. I had neglected to grab my coat, but the sweater I was wearing added some warmth. I remember feeling the cold of the night air on my face as I walked down the road away from the house. Every so often I would hear a rustle of something in the woods over my footsteps as they broke through the thin layer of hard snow beneath my feet. I would stop periodically to listen as the woods became alive with the sounds of nocturnal life, like possums, and raccoons. Every so often I would even hear the hoot of an owl in the distance.

There I was, back into the here and now, a grown man (by outward appearances); however, inside I felt like a child, who, while everyone else had moved forward, had, in fact, been left behind. I had no clear image of where I was headed with my life and could see no promise in the future. I was unsure, lost and confused. I was talking to myself in my head; however, not so much to me, but to a God that I knew I could never hope to understand. Posing questions that I longed to be answered, although I knew they wouldn't be.

I came upon a place on the road where cars could pull over if they needed to, a place I had been countless times before at many different stages in my life. It looked out over a ravine that was surrounded by tall trees in every direction. The sky was open to me as far I could see, and the stars were brilliant and thick. I found the Big Dipper easily, and as I began to search for the little one, a star streaked across the sky in one more magnificent moment of glory before ending its place amongst its fellow stars. It was an exhilarating thing to witness although not enough to calm my questions.

I stood there staring into the night, asking, what? Out loud to the universe: "What?" But "what" I didn't know. I just knew I was looking for an answer. An answer to questions I didn't even know how to ask. I don't remember any time before feeling more distraught and in discontent than on this night.

I looked out to the east, and I could see a vague appearance of a ridge line, which I knew from prior visits, was full of timber. As I gazed out, I started to notice there was a faint glow outlining the top of the ridge, it seemed to stretch out across its full length on either side adding a jagged finish to the night sky as the tree tops became more vivid.

At first I thought my mind was playing tricks on me, but as I continued to watch, the glow became bright and more apparent. I stood there confused, nervous, scared, but above all, very curious. What the heck is that? I was thinking. In that moment every scenario began to flood through my head. I thought space ship? Or maybe a hot-air balloon? I just didn't know!

Then, slowly I began to see a crest of a huge, luminescent circle, bright as anything I had ever seen and bigger than I could possibly describe.

I became aware that it was the MOON; it was HUGE and rising before me. Up over the ridge it rose, so slowly, but yet much faster than I would have thought. I was completely awestruck, and sincerely words cannot begin to even come close to describing how I felt!

I remember being more than excited and even proclaiming aloud, "Yes, YES!!!" I had never seen this before and actually never gave much thought to the fact that the moon does, in fact, rise at certain times of the year. Its brilliance cast my shadow behind me at least 20 feet, if not more. I just stood there, in awe and utter disbelief at what I was witnessing.

In that one brief moment, I knew. I knew then that things were as exactly as they should be. Right then I knew that no matter where I had been or where I was going, that I was okay, and that I always would be. It was an epiphany by every definition of the word, surreal and truly profound.

At that moment the faith that I thought I had somehow changed. It became something much different. Much BIGGER than anything I thought I had before. It was a FAITH that could move more than mountains. It was a FAITH that could move the Earth, the Moon and the entire universe. I became much smaller, and so did my troubles that night. I came away from that experience with a knowing that isn't easy to explain, but my feet became much lighter and the road much smoother from that night forward.

It was sincerely a personal experience that allows me even today to walk with a quiet confidence in knowing that I am all right where I am, and that the 'now' is the most important moment I may ever have. No matter what stage of my life I am in, even twenty years after that magnificent experience, even with all of life's ups and downs, with all its chaos and worry, I am still left with the feeling that it is truly okay to be right here right now.

I no longer have the need to compare myself with others and although that didn't change on this night, it did, in fact, set the ground work for some real personal growth, forgiveness and inevitably healing that has allowed me to feel free to be me. What an amazing gift to be free, truly free, without all the things that can potentially bind us to this Earth. Things that we are completely and solely responsible for manifesting all on our own, that we allow to hinder our growth, can easily begin to be erased in a single moment, if we are willing to let it happen.

People come and go in our lives, like the tide that takes out that which is not necessary and leaves only that which is. People not unlike the tide will come in and out leaving sometime small and sometimes large deposits within us. It is up to us to decide that which is necessary and that which isn't. Layer by layer every person, every experience, will truly define our very existence on this Earth. Alice, my father, my stepfather, teachers, siblings, co-workers, friends, and even the guy under the bridge, will make their deposits with our experience banks, and it us who will make the final decision what to do with it upon its withdrawal.

Life will happen whether you choose to participate or not, and yes! The MOON will rise, whether you are there to see it or not.

Not too long after that magnificent night when something as simple as the moon changed the course of my life; my stepfather was stricken with cancer, and it quickly claimed his life. It wasn't until years after his passing that I realized what a wonderful, caring man he was and how much of him was deposited within me which truly makes up so much of who I am.

This is my wish for you: To just feel free to be who you are in this moment, in this brief moment. That you find peace within all your experiences, and you realize that the most important experience you will have is learning to "BE" right here right now.

Thank you for allowing me to share a portion of my journey with you, and may your journey be filled with hope, peace, love and true grace always.

I would like to dedicate this story to my Stepfather, Bill. God rest his soul, a little of him lives on within me. Also my childhood friend, Alice, who accepted me for who I was and helped me realize it was okay just to be me.

My life is richer because of you both.

Thank you.

~ David Nixon

The key to realizing
a dream is to focus
not on success but on
significance – and then
even the small steps
and little victories along
your path will take on
greater meaning.

~ OPRAH WINFREY

Tammy Gynell Lagoski

Photo Credit: David Vernon

TAMMY GYNELL LAGOSKI is a published author, publishing consultant, knowledgeable in Grief Coaching and working with diverse populations. She was raised on a farm in Charleston, Illinois and currently resides in Peoria, Illinois, where she enjoys spending time with her husband, daughter, three step daughters, sons-in-law and new grand-baby. She also enjoys spending time with her two dogs, Francie and Molly, who are as rambunctious as a couple of two year olds.

tammylag@gmail.com
www.tammylagoski.com

Pebbles And Boulders

Be calm, be still, listen to the voice of the gentle soul within ... don't rush, don't panic, just be ... soon all will flow ... all will be well with thee.

~TAMMY LAGOSKI

My "Best Life" took a long time transpiring, but with the aid of a few pebbles and a boulder the size of Mt. Everest, my attention was seized. Snuggle down and prepare to follow me on a voyage into hopelessness, humiliation and a discovery of strength, faith and perseverance.

In 1998, I was working full time for the school district as a Title I Aide (working with At Risk children) and working at the public library as an assistant in both the children's and adult sections of the library. I loved both jobs, but my dream of going to college and receiving my degree was finally within my grasp. My husband's job was stable, and my daughter was active in school and busy with her friends, which enabled me to concentrate on returning to college. Alas, that was short lived as my husband decided to quit his teaching job in the middle of the fall semester, plunging us into emotional and financial chaos.

Due to our circumstances, lack of health insurance and the need to keep our home, it was imperative to find a job that would pay our bills and provide health insurance for our daughter. In our small town, jobs were hard to find that offered full-time employment, let alone insurance; consequently, I had to approach the local hog factory for a job.

Now, I want you to close your eyes and imagine a forty-something female, short, built like a round pumpkin and fifty pounds over-weight, walking into the plant for an interview. Rather picturesque isn't it! Believe it or not, I was hired to work the night shift on the line … not in the office. My new job entailed working on the "floor" where the hogs were processed; the assigned job was wielding a wizard knife which looked like a round cookie cutter, whizzing around and around while trimming the fat on the pork butts to the specified orders. The job was fast, tedious and demanding.

After about a month being on the job, I was able to transfer to another department. My new position involved wrapping pork butts and cry-ovacking the product – shoving the meat into a plastic bag, sending it down the line into a machine that sealed and extracted the air out of the product, then propelled it down the conveyer to be boxed (one example of the end product would be packaged Bacon).

The job was even faster and more complicated than wielding a knife, my body was constantly moving which was easier on the body than standing in one place and moving one arm all day long. In truth, I started to enjoy my job and along the way must have garnered the respect of my lead man as he entrusted me with the training of "new hires."

After three months of working second shift, the lead man would come over to my area and watch me wrap full shoulders. My lead man was a hard taskmaster, but a fair man. Admittedly, I was very intimidated by him, but trusted him and respected him. Not long after being on that particular job, he moved me yet again.

The new job entailed boxing the cryovacked product and throwing 70-75 pound boxes onto the conveyor line. The work area was stuck in a narrow, dreary enclosed space packed with approximately twenty bodies in a line, arms reaching out and grabbing the product, tossing it into the boxes (weight about 70-75 pounds) and sending them on their way. The robotic job continued on and on, until the end of the shift, or the line broke down which offered a brief respite.

One night, I noticed that the pace of the job kept getting faster and faster, my mind froze in a mindless state, my body and arms flaying about like a robot in high-speed motion. By the end of the shift, I could barely shuffle my way up the stairs to the locker room and then across the football field-sized parking lot to my car. Needless to say, my mind and body were totally exhausted by the time I arrived home. No way, could I sleep, so I cleaned and baked. By two in the morning I would roll into bed to sleep until it was time to get my daughter off to school.

Each night, the process continued over and over, my supervisor watching me moving around the "Pack-Off" area. I found myself becoming a bit fearful and scared wondering why I was being watched and forced to work faster and faster. A few weeks later, I discovered my supervisor was testing me for a position on day shift!!! All the hard work and watching eyes paid off … I was going to days! Believe me, this was not an easy task to accomplish for anyone, let alone an employee who had been working at the plant for three months, a rarity indeed.

My job on days entailed making boxes, wrapping picnics and full shoulders, tossing the boxes onto the line and running up and down stairs to gather more boxes. I loved the variety of the job on the Picnic line because no two days were alike which appealed to this adult with Attention Deficient Disorder (this is not said in jest, but truth).

I had been working at the plant for about five months when I discovered that the company was offering an exercise program after work. I stepped out of my comfort zone and worked out about three to four days a week at the Union Hall. When not working out at the Union Hall, I would walk two miles a day at the Park District. Before long, my hard work paid off as I dropped 50 pounds. For the first time in my life, I felt pretty and yes, even sexy.

Life at the plant went on and on ... being on line at 6:00 a.m. working hard and heading home. Sadly, after being at the plant three years, I incurred a work injury. The world turned upside down, becoming dark and bleak. Regardless of the severe pain in my hand and arm, I had to go to work each day. If I thought the physical pain was bad, that notion was soon to be short lived, as the mental and spiritual agony was soon to increase.

 Let God turn your mess into your message.

~ JOYCE MEYERS MINISTRIES

At the time of my injury, the doctors thought the pain was related to de Quervain's Disease, which is severe inflammation of the tendon in the wrist. After weeks of physical therapy, I was sent to the Orthopedic Surgeon for surgery. Sadly, the pain did not go away and, in fact, was relentless. It took a year before the actual cause was discovered and was diagnosed. In a nutshell, my disks were herniated between C-5 and C-6 and required the disks to be fused.

A couple of days after surgery, I thought I was super woman, so I proceeded in doing a few household chores; for example, unloading and loading the dishwasher, sweeping the floor and dusting. Regrettably,

I irritated my neck; thus, I had to return to the doctor's office to have him examine my neck. My poor surgeon, who had a heart of gold, restricted me to sitting, watching television and no holding books, including paperback books ... he sure knew me! I was bored, feeling sorry for myself, and crabby. I did read the paper and tried to keep up with the local news and gossip.

During my time of recovery, God decided to throw some small pebbles my way. The question was, did I notice those pebbles? Yes and no. For example, while reading the newspaper, I came across an ad for Hospice Volunteer Training. I thought to myself, "That sounds rather interesting, wouldn't mind doing something like that." But I didn't take any action.

A week later, I discovered that a church member worked for Hospice, and not long after that, my dear elderly friend was admitted to a nursing home and put on Hospice. About a week later the paper was delivered, and to my surprise the advertisement for Hospice training was still in the listings. God kept trying to get my attention by tossing tiny pebbles at me, but it took a huge boulder to finally grab my attention!

The next day, I called the Hospice Coordinator and asked her about the Volunteer Training. In turn, she explained to me what it entailed and sent me an application.

I had to get approval from my surgeon before I could attend the training because I was still in my neck collar, and my activities were restricted. When I went to see my doctor a week later, he released me ONLY to attend the Volunteer Training classes and nothing else! Not long after that, I was approved to start the training. I was ecstatic!

Training started about a month later and was it a challenge – but a good challenge. When learning about death and dying, so many emotions and spiritual issues seem to come alive. I learned more about myself than I would have imagined. Although I passed the training and received my certificate, I could not volunteer. I still had to wear my collar for awhile and await medical release.

Even though returning to work at the factory was inevitable, I dreaded it. I was still wearing my collar, and was put on "light duty" at work. In the meantime, I continued to participate in physical therapy. After being confined for so long, I decided to get out and about; therefore, I made a jaunt to a nearby town so I could run a few errands. While shopping, I had the urge to use the restroom – that is putting it mildly! As I scurried around the corner, I found myself bouncing off a tall young man. We collided with such force that it jarred and irritated my neck. I was mortified, not enough to forgo the restroom break, but enough to leave the items in my cart and head home like a mad woman.

As soon as I ran into the house, I made a frantic call to the doctor's office, and they scheduled a visit for me that day. Thankfully, only my neck muscles were jarred, and everything else remained intact. When I returned to work, I took a folder with documents detailing the incident along with the doctor's release to return to "light duty" and participate in physical therapy at the plant.

Not long after returning back to work, I was called to the Human Resource Office (HR). No one wants to be called into HR because the news is sure to be bad. Indeed it was. If you recall, I took a file into the plant regarding the incident. According to the HR gal, they never received any paper work; thus, I was accused of falsifying documents. Consequently, I was fired.

A female supervisor walked me to my locker so I could gather my personal items and then lead me out of the locker room so the plant supervisor could take over. He proceeded to walk me to the plant door. Before I exited the plant, I turned around and shook the supervisor's hand. My insides were quivering and tears threatened to explode at any moment, but I remembered the words a wise coworker and friend told me, "No matter how rough the days get, never ever show them your tears." Her words echoed inside my head as I shook plant supervisor's hands. The look on his face was one of surprise as he shook my hand and wished me well.

 ## Smile though your heart is breaking.

~TURNER AND PARSONS; NAT KING COLE

Needless to say, I wept all the way home. I cried and sobbed until I could no longer breathe. My heart was heavy, my ego destroyed. Never in my life have I been fired from a job. My spirit was broken, my faith and emotional well being shattered. What was going to happen?

I laid on the couch for days in self-pity, in rejection and humiliation. The only good thing I had going for me was Hospice. When the doctor released me back to work and placed me on light duty, my tenure as a Hospice Volunteer began. Thank God, he sent those pebbles and boulders my way. Hospice was a lifesaver. Yes, lifesaver. Visiting patients and their families gave me an insight into life that could have been so dark and bleak, but instead I found light. My heart opened and was filled with joy and peace with each visit made to my patients. It is hard to focus on self when watching someone who is suffering vicious pain and facing death with a sense of calmness and peace.

A year went by, life was improving, but something was about to happen that would affirm that I was worthy, not a failure or a loser. Three events would transpire in fairly quick succession. The first major event was exoneration from the plant regarding the falsification of documents; the paper work had been located thus, my name was exonerated. What a joy. I felt so happy, so free and light.

The second event that happened was the job of Hospice Volunteer Coordinator. I applied for the job, and God granted me the position. He was showing me I was worthy, faithful and deserving despite my lack of faith and neglect during my darkest hour.

Lastly, the library where I had been employed since 1982 as a librarian's assistant (except for about four years I did not work there) had an opening for the Director. My mentor had decided to retire. Nervously, I submitted a resume, and along with 10 applicants was interviewed by the nine-member board. If memory serves me correctly, most of the applicants had Bachelor's degrees, Master's degrees and/or a Master of Library Science degree, but I only had a couple years of college and plethora of experience.

Once again, God looked down upon me and bestowed upon me another blessing … the Directorship of the library. My self-esteem grew, and I discovered that I was capable of doing many things that I would never have dared to try before I lost my job at the plant. Some day, I will tell you all about that wonderful adventure in my life. Until then, I would like to share with you the definition of the word "best":

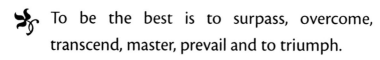 To be the best is to surpass, overcome, transcend, master, prevail and to triumph.

~ MERRIAM-WEBSTER'S COLLEGIATE THESAURUS

Life is always moving, the soul and mind always growing; therefore, one has the advantage of creating and stepping into their best life on a daily basis; in essence to overcome the pebbles and boulders in one's life, to prevail upon life's travails.

To my grandmother, my mother and aunt who are akin to Lucy and Ethel, and my daughter, Mara. Toss us together, and we become a mass of laughter and tears. Chuck, thank you for loving me and accepting the quirky lady that I am. I love you more than infinity.

Alice Lou Gramann, thank you for mentoring and believing in me. Because of you, I fulfilled my dream of becoming a Librarian. To Mary Downing, my dear friend and mentor. Mary, thank you for believing in me, guiding me and supporting me throughout the years. To Karen Egan for encouraging me to "Think Outside the Box."

Lastly, thank you to the Illinois State Librarians, who are dedicated to serving the patrons and libraries under their tutelage. I admire and respect you all ...

~ Tammy Gynell Lagoski

Lindsley Silagi

Photo Credit: Cindy Lee

LINDSLEY SILAGI is an Educator and Professional Coach with a private coaching practice, Step By Step Results!, in Santa Teresa, New Mexico where she lives happily with her husband. She conducts healing and motivational workshops and retreats to help others release and let go of lack and limitation, "get into flow," and to connect with their soul's calling.

Lindsley loves dance, art, people, photography, travel. And most of all she loves to share a great laugh with a friend.

lindsley.silagi@gmail.com
www.stepbystepresults.net

❧ Step In, Do Step In

If I have belief that I can do it, I shall surely
acquire the capacity to do it, even if I do not
have it at the beginning.

~MAHATMA GANDHI

The Invitation

Come forward into your Best Life. Come into the Life that you were meant to live. Sign up here. It begins the moment you decide to choose to participate. You were born for living this life, as your best life. You were born for greatness. If you are reading this and you are yearning for more in life, for more out of life, pay attention. That yearning is the **S**pirit, the **T**ruth, the **E**nergy, and the **P**ower within you that is calling to you. It is calling to you and it is for you alone to answer. This is your invitation, your invitation to **STEP** in.

So How Do You Do It?

My advice: just take one step. And then another. The important thing is to begin. Choose a new thought. And then another. In this way you may begin to step into your best life. It will not happen all at once. It is a process. And in the process you will discover excitement, joy, wonder, happiness, love, peace, fulfillment. You will experience fear, loneliness, self-doubt, and judgment, too. These are not to be avoided but rather to be faced. When you do face these beliefs, which are false beliefs, it will free you to experience more, express more, and accomplish more.

In order to face the fears that you may hold, and the beliefs that you may have, it requires that you are willing to examine them. Are you willing? A willingness to shift from your old limited ways of being and a willingness to let go of your fears is required. But how? How do you move yourself out of the beliefs that have kept you living the only way you know?

I offer you three steps to move you onward. I myself take these three steps daily to open myself up to experiencing more, and stepping into My Best Life.

I allow. I ask. I affirm.

These I practice consciously. I offer them to you to start you on your pathway. Let me share how to begin.

Allow

Allow yourself to experience more of what you desire in life by stepping into what you truly want to take in to be your life. Just take a step forward. One step is all you need to get yourself moving. Allow yourself to grow. What do you want to learn? What do you want to do? What do you want to experience? Get started. Make a call. Sign up for a class. Write a proposal. Travel someplace you have never been. Make a move. It is yours to make.

Perhaps you are afraid you will make a mistake. If this is the case, if you are afraid to make a mistake, this is a thought that bears examination, as it will hold you back from experiencing the life you desire. Ask: "Where did this thought come from?" Begin here. This thought is one to eliminate. You do this by **letting go**. It sounds simple and it is, when you are ready. Recognize the fear, and then, let go. Simply, allow the thought to go. Shift away from this limited belief that you need to be perfect. Instead, allow yourself to make mistakes. Allow these mistakes to be just stepping stones along the way.

Do you judge yourself? Do you criticize yourself? If you do, these are two habits to eliminate from your life. Give up the judgment and criticism of self. This will require conscious effort to eliminate if you have had a long- standing habit of self-criticism. It is worth the effort. As you let go, you allow in at the same time. Focus your attention on what you allow in when you stop the judgment and criticism. Allow for imperfection as you create the pathway for your journey to unfold.

The practice of allowing requires tools. One tool that is helpful in making your shift in mindset is affirmation. You may discover that you need more patience, more determination, more enthusiasm, more love, more energy, more consistent effort, more persistence, more skill, simply more of what you perceive you lack. Begin a practice of daily affirmation to claim that which you desire and that which you determine you need.

When you discover that you need more of one thing or another, your first thought may be one of discouragement, disappointment, self-doubt, or fear. You may become impatient or even confused. It is helpful to recognize that these emotions are going to show up and that they are a normal part of the change process. Do not let these emotions deter you. Consider them a part of the pathway to your greater and greater success. Acknowledge these emotions. They are reminders of the importance of taking the step of allowing. By doing this you can shift the state of your mind and the state of your heart.

You were born for greatness, and you will experience this greatness when you allow more. Allow yourself to let go of the need to know all the answers. Give up the need to be right. Allow yourself to step into the unknown territory and trust. Research in the fields of psychology, neuroscience, and quantum physics all indicate that human potential is mostly a result of habitual thinking and thought patterns than anything else.

So allow yourself to grow. Allow yourself to grow to be who you desire to be. Allow yourself to be a giver. Allow yourself to be a receiver. Allow yourself to get into a flow state. Allow for joy. Allow for greater joy. Allow yourself to be grateful. Allow your gratitude to grow. Allow the true genius that lives inside of you to awaken from within.

Do this through affirmation. Affirm: "I now allow myself to grow." Or, "I now allow myself to be more giving." Or, "I now allow myself to be in joyfulness." Or, "I now allow myself to be enthusiastic." Or, "I now allow for the spirit of discovery to be my guide." Be creative.

Most of all allow kindness into your daily living. It is only through being kind to yourself that your genius will emerge. Be kind to yourself and allow the imperfections just to be there. Work on developing new skill sets one step at a time and then recognize yourself for the progress you are making.

Ask

Ask yourself questions. Teach yourself to ask questions of yourself. This will open you up to wonder and to realize that there is so much more than the perspective you have held onto until now. It is important to use open-ended questions as these will activate your thinking and thus set you up for growing, for learning.

Become more of who you are by taking the step to ask. All of us build our set of beliefs as we experience life. Some of these beliefs are consciously held beliefs. Others may be beliefs of which we are not aware.

We may be blinded to our beliefs and think that the way we think is real, is reality. As we learn to question ourselves, to question whether what we think and believe is true, we start to see how a shift in our perspective changes things for us.

Here are some questions you may want to use to get started. Suppose you have the belief that you do not have enough time. Ask yourself, "What if I decided I do have enough time?" By asking yourself this question, you are taking the step to shift your perspective on your belief. Other questions like these may then follow: "What might I need to do to create the time that I need to accomplish this goal?" Or, "What might I need to give up to allow myself more time to devote to this goal of mine?"

Suppose you believe you do not have enough money to accomplish the goal. Ask yourself, "How might I get the money I need? What step might I need to take? Who might support me to take this step?" Continue to challenge your beliefs by asking questions.

Ask yourself: "Why am I? Why am I doing this in this way? Why am I taking the route I take to work?" Then ask, "Why not change it? Why not go on a new route, go in a new direction?" Asking yourself questions in this way opens you up and stimulates your creative thinking. Try it out.

Another great starter for shifting a belief is: "If not now ... when? If not now ...when will I take action on that big lofty goal?" The important thing is to inquire in order to discover what is holding you back. By asking yourself this question and other similar questions, you begin to develop a greater self-understanding at the conscious level. You begin to come into knowing a greater truth. You will begin to recognize that you are the one who holds yourself back. No one else. And once you recognize this, you are on the pathway to a greater freedom, a greater joy, and a greater fulfillment.

It is also helpful to ask for guidance. So begin a practice of asking for guidance. Ask for willingness. Ask for acceptance. Ask for forgiveness. Ask for strength. Ask for kindness. Ask for help in letting go. Ask for help. Then experience these in your life as you receive them. I want to make a special note here. As you recognize that you are receiving, that you are in receipt of what you have asked for, it is important to say thank you. Take time each day to be grateful for all you have. Then watch as your gratitude grows. It is through taking a positive, an affirmative stance, one that allows more, and judges less, that will result in an abundance of things for which to be grateful. So take time each day to ask. And take time each day to say thank you.

Affirm

As I have mentioned earlier, affirmation is a helpful tool to shift your mindset. Now let's look at affirmation more closely. When you begin to learn a new skill or process, you are bound to be less than perfect. Affirmation is important so that you do not give up particularly when you are at the beginning, just getting started on making the very changes that will make a difference in your outcomes. Affirmation supports you. Self-criticism does the opposite. By turning your thoughts to the positive, you will have a positive effect in the change process. Affirm yourself. Use the present tense when creating your affirmations. Here are a few samples to use. Say them out loud with feeling. Better yet, sing them out loud with feeling. Try a few of the positive, present-tense affirmations that follow:

> *I am open. I am loving and kind. I am giving and forgiving. I am a success. I am a winner. I am living an amazing and joy-filled life. I am calm and confident. I love life and life loves me. I am happy and living my best life now.*

Five to ten repetitions a session is all you need. Plan to do three sessions a day. Make room for this in your life. It will only take five to ten minutes, three times a day to change your thinking. Make a commitment to this process. Commit to this practice for 21 days. This commitment will provide you with the energy you need to make it happen. Place this practice at the top of your list of daily actions. By making a conscious effort this will become a sustained daily practice over time and you will develop a more positive, self-affirming way of thinking that will benefit and serve you.

Although this sounds simple, it requires effort and persistence to establish this positive habit in your life. It is worth your effort. Affirmation helps you "let go" or eliminate something in your life no longer needed and helps you invite something new into your life that you desire. By choosing to step into the conscious use of affirmation, you are setting a course for your greater success.

Once you work with affirmation long enough it will become a way of thinking. You will find that your whole outlook on life shifts, and you will begin to recognize that you are creating and experiencing Your Best Life *now*.

So begin today. Allow more. Ask more. Affirm more.

Allow. Ask. Affirm.

In this way may you discover as I have, how to be, how to do, and how to have what you want in your life. We are the only ones who can create the desired changes in our lives. *It is up to us.* It takes consistent effort and persistent action. It takes developing a support system. It takes patience and ability to be grateful for your place on your journey.

It takes maintaining care of the self. It takes courage commitment and a knowing determination. Do follow your heart. Pay attention to it as it will lead the way if you listen. Do not allow your light to be dimmed. Allow it to shine brightly. Answer your own calling. You are moving forward dear reader. There is no turning back now.

Be open to life, to living it richly, and it will be open to you.

Note: All content here was written by Lindsley in the wee hours of the morning while cruising down the Yangtze River in the Chongqing Province of China during the final days of March 2012.

To Help Others On The Journey Of This Life

Thank you to all who have touched my life.

You do know who you are.

And because of you I know myself more fully.

~ Lindsley Silagi

Mavis Hogan

MAVIS HOGAN is a business owner and event coordinator, living in Spokane, WA. She is also a certified Reflexologist and Reiki Master. Mavis is a lifelong student of the metaphysical and relishes the journey and all the people who touch her life. She enjoys reading, writing, and spending time with her three kids and six grandchildren.

mavishogan@comcast.net

Bricks In The Wall Of Who You Become

 Are you questioning whether what you think, say or do has no value? Then Stop!

Your opinions count, your words matter and your actions make a difference.

Through the lives you touch, you make this world a better place. Thank goodness you're here.

It wouldn't be the same without you!

~ UNKNOWN

How many times throughout our lives do we stop and wonder why we did what we did? Or, do what we do. Or, perhaps meet the people we met or go the places we went?

What exactly got us to this point in our life, and where do we go from here?

You may not understand it yet, but the things you do, the people you know and the places you go, all of it, are bricks in your wall.

Many times I would look back over my life and ponder these very questions. Why was I given the family that I had? Why did I make the friends that I made? Why did I marry the men that I did and have the children I had?

Better yet, was I a good daughter, sister, wife, mother and friend? Did I instill values in my children that will help make them better people, parents, wives or husband? Will people's lives be changed for having known me?

I think everyone asks themselves these questions. We are all searching for the answers in our own lives.

I believe that we chose our lives. We made a plan to come here, and we set the plan into motion. We have an outline, so to speak.

So we are born and life begins.

As we go on through our life, the things that happen along the way, the day-to-day stuff, are what I refer to as the Bricks in the wall of who we become.

The Dash

There is a story that I read once about a person who was dying, and he asked his friend to read something at his funeral. The title of what he read was called "The Dash." It is the story of a person's life written on their tombstone. We all have a beginning, the day we were born. We all have an ending, the day that we die, but it is the (-) between those two dates that mean so much more.

How you live *YOUR* Dash is what is important.

My life as most people's, was spent the way *other* people thought I should live, beginning with my parents. As we know, most parents want only the best for their children, or so we hope. Others are not so fortunate. They may get a bummer life. So here come your first Bricks. You are raised by people who already have a belief system in place, and after all you are their child, so they can mold you how they see fit. You came here with other ideas perhaps. But because you are the child, you must be molded and formed for the life *they* envision. The hardest part, I think, is to accept your parents as students of the classroom of life, just as you yourself are. They did the best they could from where they came, just as you will do the best you can from where you come.

And so it begins.

So you grow and develop. You now have parents, siblings, teachers and friends. All of them are adding bricks to your wall just by being in your life. They are sharing with you their thoughts and beliefs, actions and knowledge, and as you listen, you are forming new ideas, based on concepts that you have heard from others. Some will make you change your mind, while others convince you of the very opposite. They are feeding you the information which you will piece together and create your "Dash." As you get older, you begin to see how other people live, and you know that you may want what they have or that you definitely do NOT. More Bricks.

You are given choices and options in life. You are growing and spreading your wings. Some choose to marry. Some choose further education. Some pack up and head out on a trek around the world. The world is your arena. Whatever you choose to do is an adventure. But no matter what you choose to do, you will see things, smell things, taste things, and experience things that will be with you the rest of your life. There will be fun things and sad things. There will be love and fear. There will be pain. But all will be YOUR bricks. No one will carry them the same way you do. These are your bricks. You can carry them or put them down, it is your choice, but they will form you into the person you become.

Whatever adventure you create for yourself sets you on the path of where you are headed. You don't know it yet, but the course you have set into motion is only the beginning.

The Journey To "There"

When you are young, you are so eager to get there. Wherever *"There"* is. You are on a mission to get there and get there fast. But somewhere along the way they forgot to tell us, there is no *There*. There is no magical age where you say, "There, I am here. I have arrived."

When I was young, it was all about being 18 and out of the house and on my own. I didn't look any further than that. My life was boring living at home, and I had places to go and things to do. So, I chose to get married at 18 and have babies. I was going to be the best mom and raise the happiest family. I knew what that should look like because I knew what I had wanted and didn't have. So I would create it. I knew I had the bricks I needed, but I didn't realize that not everyone's bricks blended together. I was more alone and lonely being married than I had been living with my parents. They (the parents) had tried to warn me, but I wouldn't listen.

Here comes another brick, the one about learning your own lessons. You cannot tell anyone how to live their life, you cannot take away the things that make someone's life tough, nor can you warn them of impending doom. Or even tell them what will make them happy. They will not hear you. We all must learn from our own mistakes and choices. To hear how my mother lived had nothing to do with my life. That was hers. Those were the "old" days. This was a new time, and I was going to do it better and different. It was different but it was not better. To try to tell my kids that today only falls on deaf ears as well. They, too, have to do it their way.

So, I went from parents that I thought didn't understand me, to a husband I *knew* didn't. Again I found myself in a situation of someone trying to control my life. But this time, I wasn't bored – I was scared most of the time as he made my life miserable. I should have paid attention on one of our earliest dates when he informed me that marriage was like a spider web: He was the spider, and the wife was the fly. I thought that surely he was teasing me. But it turned out to be a good analogy of what was to come in my not-too-distant future.

He controlled my life with fear. I had no money. I made no choices. He dictated everything from when I could watch TV to what I could wear. To when I could drive the car, or visit with friends, to when I could leave the house or when to stay home, to when to find a job or when to quit.

I was not free to leave the house without permission. I could not drive the car without following his rules, and he kept track of mileage on the car and made me account for each mile. The drapes were kept closed. The towels in the bathroom must hang straight. No wrinkles in the bedspread. Dinner must be served at the appropriate time, and if there was no real food to eat, I *would* make something from next to nothing. Most of the time there was no phone.

When we would fight he would spend the night sitting beside me poking me awake every time I fell asleep. When I felt like I couldn't breathe anymore, I was told I couldn't make it without him, I wasn't smart enough to go it on my own, and I believed him. Where was I going to go anyway?

If you are not being treated with love & respect, check your "price tag." Perhaps you have marked yourself down. It's you who tell people what you're worth by what you accept. Get off of the "clearance rack" and get behind the glass where they keep all the "valuables."

~UNKNOWN

Getting Off The Clearance Rack

My married life had been miserable for four years. I had been mistreated physically and emotionally. When that started to happen to my children as well, I knew it was time to leave. I had not made the choice to save myself up to that point, but I *would* save my children.

I woke up one morning and knew this was the day I would leave. The funny thing was, there had been no fighting or screaming. No battle that day. I had reached the end of my rope. I was just done, and this was the day. I was about to find out just how strong I could be.

I had recently had major ear surgery and needed to see the doctor for a follow up visit in only a couple of days. I didn't care. We had recently moved into a new home, in a new town, and I didn't know where we were exactly. I didn't care. I couldn't have given anyone directions to come get me. We didn't have a phone. I had no access to a car. I didn't care about any of that. This was the day.

It was raining, and I remember asking God to make it quit. That would be my sign that I was doing the right thing. (People are so funny. We know what we want, but we need a sign to make it okay when all you need to do is give *Yourself* permission.)

I had two small children, and I needed to try to get the courage to go next door to ask to use a phone to call for help. I was so scared. It kept raining. Again I begged, "God, if I am supposed to leave, make it quit raining. That will be my sign." It kept raining. Yet I knew I couldn't possibly be meant to continue to live like this so, with or without God's help, or a sign, I was determined to make a new choice for us that day.

I put the baby in her bed for a nap, locked the door and took my son with me next door. I was so scared, but I knocked on the door and asked to use the phone. I told them it would have to be long distance, but I would make sure they weren't charged. They gave me the phone and left the room (bless their hearts) and let me make my call. I called my sister and told her I needed help. She lived four hours away, but I told her where to come find me knowing I had four hours to figure out how to get there. I thanked the people for the use of their phone and went home to pack.

I had two paper bags that I filled with a change of clothes for us and stuff for the baby. I had no idea what I was going to do, but I was packed. But, I knew I couldn't just walk out. First of all I had no idea which way to go. Second of all, a baby and a three year old and two paper bags? Seriously? I was going to need Divine intervention of some kind.

I went and sat in the living room to make a plan, and as I sat there contemplating my escape and our future, my husband pulled up in front of the house. He never came home for lunch. Why was he here today? When he came into the house, my son said in a happy voice, "Dad, do you want to see how we are all packed?" Then took him in the bedroom and showed him the two paper bags. When my husband came out he looked at me and said, "I am going back to work, are you going to be here when I get home?" I said I didn't know. (I didn't *want* to be, didn't *plan* to be, but was too scared of him to say so.)

Five minutes after he left, my very special "auntie" in the whole world came over. She had never visited here before. Why was she here today? Inside me I knew that surely God had sent her. Here was my sign. Here was my way out. I begged her to take me to my friend's house where I had told my sister to find me. It took a little persuading – okay, a lot of persuading. I had never told anyone that my husband and I had problems, so it came as a shock to her that I was running away.

I have to say that although I convinced her to take me, we didn't talk again for two years (a big brick) because she thought I was wrong. At the time, I forgave her silently because I knew she didn't have all the information, and I hadn't had the time to fill her in. (We would eventually make up.) She took me to my friend's house, and my sister eventually arrived. And the rest as they say, is history! Oh, the bricks in that story. The scared little girl who grew up that day!

I admitted defeat with that particular life lesson, and moved 300 miles back home with my parents until I could get on my feet.

I found a place for us to live, and I can remember one of the first things I did in our new home was change an outlet cover on the wall. And I cried from happiness that yes, I could make it without *him*, look at what I had just accomplished. I CHANGED AN OUTLET COVER! It may sound silly in the repeating, but I was so proud at the time! And that one small step was the first of many that helped me begin to trust that I was going to be okay.

 And the day came when the risk it took to remain tight in a bud was more painful that the risk it took to blossom.

~ANAIS NIN

Free To Find My Way

As I began to create a new life for the three of us, I realized that I was stepping away from a life where I had been controlled by someone. Now I was NEVER, *to the best of my ability*, going to accept that kind of control again. I would learn how to take care of myself and my children, and we would make our own memories. I had been made to feel a prisoner in my own home for years. I felt I was not able to make decisions or choices without someone else's approval. That was now going to change.

After I was strong enough to escape that life, I knew what I *didn't* want. I had been controlled enough for one life time. My bricks had started crumbling, but I was going to rebuild. (One day many years later I would be able to forgive that life and that boy. After all, he had his bricks as well and did what he had known to do from his life lessons. I was never one for revenge, but there is a saying that the best revenge is living a great life and being happy. And, that is just what I have done!)

I won't say it was easy, but I was free. Free to find my way. Free to build my life as I chose. Free to have to answer only to myself. The best lessons learned are the ones we learn by our own choices. There is no one who knows what you need or desire, only you. You alone create your reality. You will make decisions that affect the rest of your life, and you will wonder why you made that choice. It is all about becoming YOU. The best YOU, you can be.

The Older I Get, The Better I Like Me And My Life!

Each of us is here to learn, to love and to grow, whether it is from our mistakes or from the things that go well, from the books we read, from people we meet or from the Universe itself. I now know that the answer is, All of the Above. Stepping into the best possible life you can, anyway you can.

Those bricks that you started out with created your foundation, whether they were sturdy bricks on which to build, or crumbly bricks that toppled over, they were your beginning. As you learned more about YOU, you added new layers. The beauty of it all is you can make changes at any time. Try a new fork in the road. Take the road less traveled or take the paved way. Your bricks are like stepping stones to where you're going. If your foundation crumbled, make a new one, it's never too late to start again.

As you get stronger and start to trust yourself and others, you will do new things and meet new people. You will hear things or see things that continue to mortar up those bricks. Life is not a race about getting THERE, wherever there is, it is about the journey, the process, the living: "The Bricks."

Dedicated to all the people, places and things which have contributed "Bricks" to my wall.

Because of you ... I am!

Thank you to my family and friends who are always there for me, and to the ones who no longer are. You all have a special place in my heart (some of you a little extra). To those who read my words, I hope they touched you in some small way or gave you a connection that someone knows how you feel. To Nancy, I am glad we found each other on that "street corner," and I can't wait to see what other journeys life has in store for us. Here's to the next bricks!

~ Mavis Hogan

The first step towards
getting somewhere
is to decide that you
are not going to stay
where you are.

~ JOHN PIERPONT MORGAN

Resources

The following list of resources are for the national headquarters; search in your yellow pages under "Community Services" for your local resource agencies and support groups.

AIDS

CDC National AIDS Hotline
(800) 342-2437

ALCOHOL ABUSE

Al-Anon Family Group Headquarters
1600 Corporate Landing Parkway
Virginia Beach, VA 23454-5617
(888) 4AL-ANON
www.al-anon.alateen.org

Alcoholics Anonymous (AA)
General Service Office
475 Riverside Dr., 11th Floor
New York, NY 10115
(212) 870-3400
www.alcoholics-anonymous.org

Children of Alcoholics Foundation
164 W. 74th Street
New York, NY 10023
(800) 359-COAF
www.coaf.org

Mothers Against Drunk Driving
MADD
P.O. Box 541688
Dallas, TX 75354
(800) GET-MADD
www.madd.org

National Association of Children of Alcoholics (NACoA)
11426 Rockville Pike, #100
Rockville, MD 20852
(888) 554-2627
www.nacoa.net

Women for Sobriety
P.O. Box 618
Quartertown, PA 18951
(215) 536-8026
www.womenforsobriety.org

CHILDREN'S RESOURCES

Child Molestation

ChildHelp USA/Child Abuse Hotline
15757 N. 78th St.
Scottsdale, AZ 85260
(800) 422-4453
www.childhelpusa.org

Prevent Child Abuse America
200 South Michigan Avenue, 17th Floor
Chicago, IL 60604
(312) 663-3520
www.preventchildabuse.org

Crisis Intervention

Girls and Boys Town National Hotline
(800) 448-3000
www.boystown.org

Children's Advocacy Center of East Central Illinois
*(If your heart feels directed to make a donation to this center,
please include Lisa Hardwick's name in the memo)*
616 6th Street
Charleston, IL 61920
(217) 345-8250
http://caceci.org

Children of the Night
14530 Sylvan St.
Van Nuys, CA 91411
(800) 551-1300
www.childrenofthenight.org

National Children's Advocacy Center
210 Pratt Avenue
Huntsville, AL 35801
(256) 533-KIDS (5437)
www.nationalcac.org

Co-Dependency

Co-Dependents Anonymous
P.O. Box 33577
Phoenix, AZ 85067
(602) 277-7991
www.codependents.org

Suicide, Death, Grief

AARP Grief and Loss Programs
(800) 424-3410
www.aarp.org/griefandloss

Grief Recovery Institute
P.O. Box 6061-382
Sherman Oaks, CA 91413
(818) 907-9600
www.grief-recovery.com

Suicide Awareness Voices of Education
Minneapolis, MN 55424
(952) 946-7998

Suicide National Hotline
(800) 784-2433

DOMESTIC VIOLENCE

National Coalition Against Domestic Violence
P.O. Box 18749
Denver, CO 80218
(303) 831-9251
www.ncadv.org

National Domestic Violence Hotline
P.O. Box 161810
Austin, TX 78716
(800) 799-SAFE
www.ndvh.org

DRUG ABUSE

Cocaine Anonymous National Referral Line
(800) 347-8998

National Helpline of Phoenix House
(800) COCAINE
www.drughelp.org

National Institute of Drug Abuse
(NIDA)
6001 Executive Blvd., Room 5213,
Bethesda, MD 20892-9561, Parklawn
Building
Info: (301) 443-6245
Help: (800) 662-4357
www.nida.nih.gov

EATING DISORDERS

Overeaters Anonymous
National Office
P.O. Box 44020
Rio Rancho, NM 87174-4020
(505) 891-2664
www.overeatersanonymous.org

GAMBLING

Gamblers Anonymous
International Service Office
P.O. Box 17173
Los Angeles, CA 90017
(213) 386-8789
www.gamblersanonymous.org

HEALTH ISSUES

American Chronic Pain Association
P.O. Box 850
Rocklin, CA 95677
(916) 632-0922
www.theacpa.org

American Holistic Health Association
P.O. Box 17400
Anaheim, CA 92817
(714) 779-6152
www.ahha.org

The Chopra Center at La Costa Resort and Spa Deepak Chopra, M.D.
2013 Costa Del Mar
Carlsbad, CA 92009
(760) 494-1600
www.chopra.com

The Mind-Body Medical Institute
110 Francis St., Ste. 1A
Boston, MA 02215
(617) 632-9530 Ext. 1
www.mbmi.org

National Health Information Center
P.O. Box 1133
Washington, DC 20013-1133
(800) 336-4797
www.health.gov/NHIC

Preventive Medicine Research Institute
Dean Ornish, M.D.
900 Brideway, Ste 2
Sausalito, CA 94965
(415) 332-2525
www.pmri.org

MENTAL HEALTH

American Psychiatric Association of America
1400 K St. NW
Washington, DC 20005
(888) 357-7924
www.psych.org

Anxiety Disorders Association of America
11900 Parklawn Dr., Ste. 100
Rockville, MD 20852
(310) 231-9350
www.adaa.org

The Help Center of the American Psychological Association
(800) 964-2000
www.helping.apa.org

National Center for Post Traumatic Stress Disorder
(802) 296-5132
www.ncptsd.org

National Alliance for the Mentally Ill
2107 Wilson Blvd., Ste. 300
Arlington, VA 22201
(800) 950-6264
www.nami.org

National Depressive and Manic-Depressive Association
730 N. Franklin St., Ste. 501
Chicago, IL 60610
(800) 826-3632
www.ndmda.org

National Institute of Mental Health
6001 Executive Blvd.
Room 81884, MSC 9663
Bethesda, MD 20892
(301) 443-4513
www.nimh.nih.gov

SEX ISSUES

Rape, Abuse and Incest
National Network
(800) 656-4673
www.rainn.org

National Council on Sexual Addiction
and Compulsivity
P.O. Box 725544
Atlanta, GA 31139
(770) 541-9912
www.ncsac.org

SMOKING

Nicotine Anonymous World Services
419 Main St., PMB #370
Huntington Beach, CA 92648
(415) 750-0328
www.nicotine-anonymous.org

STRESS ISSUES

The Biofeedback & Psychophysiology Clinic
The Menninger Clinic
P.O. Box 829
Topeka, KS 66601-0829
(800) 351-9058
www.menninger.edu

New York Open Center
83 Spring St.
New York, NY 10012
(212) 219-2527
www.opencenter.org

The Stress Reduction Clinic Center for Mindfulness
University of Massachusetts
Medical Center
55 Lake Ave., North
Worcester, MA 01655
(508) 856-2656

TEEN

Al-Anon/Alateen
1600 Corporate Landing Parkway
Virginia Beach, VA 23454-5617
(888) 425-2666
www.al-anon.alateen.org

Planned Parenthood
810 Seventh Ave.
New York, NY 10019
(800) 230-PLAN
www.plannedparenthood.org

Hotlines for Teenagers
Girls and Boys Town National Hotline
(800) 448-3000

ChildHelp National Child Abuse Hotline
(800) 422-4453

Just for Kids Hotline
(888) 594-KIDS

National Child Abuse Hotline
(800) 792-5200

National Runaway Hotline
(800) 621-4000

National Youth Crisis Hotline
(800)-HIT-HOME

Suicide Prevention Hotline
(800) 827-7571

🌿 Bibliography

Beckwith , Michael Bernard.
"The Life Visioning Process"

Benson, Herbert. (1975).
The Relaxation Response.
New York, NY. Harper Torch

The Success Principles: How to Get from Where You Are to Where You
Want to Be.
New York, NY: Collins
Chopra, Deepak, M.D. (1990.)

Choquette, Sonia.
The Answer Is Simple... Love yourself, Live your Spirit
Hay House

Cohen, Alan.
"Create A Masterpiece; When mistakes turn into miracles."
healyourlife.com. N.p., 31 Dec. 2010. Web. 13 Mar. 2011.

Crane, Patricia J. (2002.)
Ordering From the Cosmic Kitchen:
The Essential Guide to Powerful, Nourishing Affirmations. Bonsall,
CA. The Crane's Nest.

Gilbert, Daniel. (2005).
Stumbling on Happiness.
New York, NY. Vintage

Gilligan, Stephen. (1997).
The Courage to Love: Principles and
Practices of Self-Relations Psychotherapy.
New York, NY. W.W. Norton &Company

Goleman, Daniel. (1995).
Emotional Intelligence: Why it can matter more than IQ. New York,
NY: Bantam Dell

Hay, Louise L.
(1982.) Heal Your Body. Carlsbad, CA. Hay House, Inc.
(1984.) You Can Heal Your Life. Carlsbad, CA. Hay House, Inc.
(2002.) You Can Heal Your Life Companion Book. Carlsbad, CA. Hay
House, Inc.
(1991.) The Power Is Within You. Carlsbad, CA. Hay House, Inc.

"Inspirational Quotations by Alan Cohen."
alancohen.com. N.p., n.d. Web. 13 Mar. 2011.

Landrum, Gene. (2005).
The Superman Syndrome: You Are What You Believe.
Lincoln, NE. iUniverse

Lesser, Elizabeth.
Broken Open.
N.p.: Random House, 2005. Print

Lipton, Bruce H., Ph.D. (2005.)
The Biology of Belief: Unleashing the Power of Consciousness,
Matter & Miracles. Carlsbad, CA.
Hay House, Inc.194

Millman, Dan.
The Life You Were Born To Live. Tiburon, CA:
HJ Kramer Inc, 1993. Print.

Moat, Richard. Moativational Medicine ™

Morrissey, Mary. N.p.: n.p., 2009
Life Solutions That Work, LLC. Print.

Neill, Michael. (2006).
You Can Have What You Want:
Proven Strategies for Inner and Outer Success.
Hay House

Tolle, Eckhart. (1999.)
The Power of Now: A Guide to Spiritual Enlightenment. Novato, CA.
New World Library.
A New Earth: awakening to Your Life's Purpose.
N.p.: Plume, 2008. Print.

Truman, Karol.
Feelings Buried Alive Never Die. Las Vegas, NV:
Olympus Distributing, 1991. Print.

Wolinsky, Stephen. (1991).
Trances People Live:
Healing Approaches In Quantum Psychology.
Falls Village, CT. The Bramble Company

Williamson, Marianne. (2009).
The Age of Miracles: Embracing the New Midlife.
Carlsbad, CA. Hay House

❧ A Call For Authors

Most people have a story that needs to be shared – could **YOU** be one of the contributing authors we are seeking to feature in one of our upcoming books?

Whether you envision yourself participating in an inspiring book with other authors, or whether you have a dream of writing your very own book, we may be the answer **YOU** have been searching for!

Are you interested in experiencing how sharing your message will assist with building your business network, which in turn will result in being able to assist even more people? Or perhaps you are interested in leaving a legacy for your family and friends? Or it may be you simply have an important message your heart is telling you to share with the world. Each person has their own unique reason for desiring to become an author.

Our commitment is to make this planet we call "home" a better place. One of the ways we fulfill this commitment is assisting others in sharing their inspiring messages.

We look forward to hearing from you.

Please visit us at

www.visionaryinsightpress.com

CPSIA information can be obtained at www.ICGtesting.com
Printed in the USA
LVOW101000180313

324546LV00007B/37/P